AMONG FRIENDS

The Best of
MIKE HARDEN

TO RICK,
WITH ALL
THE BEST OF WISHES.
Milw Cohen
—1995

ENJOY!

For Sam Perdue

Acknowledgements

All columns appearing in this book were previously published in The *Columbus Dispatch*. They are reprinted here with the permission of the paper. The author thanks *The Dispatch* for allowing him to print a second time what they have already paid him once for writing.

Special thanks to my brother, Dan, for tirelessly shepherding this collection through its various phases. His company, Image Assembly, contributed greatly to its overall quality.

Thanks, also, to The Prep Department Graphics, Billie Patterson and Linda Rathburn for quality work under the gun.

My appreciation to Ron Slone and Byrum Lithographing Co. Who said that boy couldn't do anything but pick and sing?

Thanks to Mary Circelli for unselfishly sharing her time, efforts and considerable photographic talents.

Finally, for their experience, strength and hope (not to mention friendship), I am grateful to the friends of Bill W.

Wing & Prayer Publishers
First Printing: November, 1993

Contents

BOOKS BY MIKE HARDEN

Passage to America
First Gathering
Playing Favorites
Fight for Life
Homegrown
Heartland Journal
Among Friends

"Column Helper"

October 28, 1990

Through the years, many of you have written to me asking, "Mike, how do you ever manage to fill all of that space four times a week?"

Friends, I couldn't do it without General Mills Column Helper. You have, perhaps, used a similar product in the kitchen when in-laws drop in an hour before dinner and all you have is a pound of ground round or a can of tuna.

Column Helper is a blend of word extenders, asides, reminiscences, digressions, useless modifiers, parenthetical explanations of the obvious, florid adjectives and other people's quotations that make it possible to take what doesn't deserve more than a paragraph and stretch it into a column.

Permit me to offer a small example.

Let's say I am writing a column about doing handiwork around the house. I get to the part where I smack my thumb with the hammer. Without Column Helper, I would yell, "Ow!" But "ow" has only two letters. Watch what happens when you add Column Helper.

I brought the hammer back and swung with all my might.

"Arrrrrrrrrrrrrrrrrrrrrrgh!" I yelled. "That hurt!"

Now try it one more time, fleshing it out even more with useless modifiers, filler and a worthless parenthetical explanation of the obvious:

I brought the hammer (which I was using to drive nails) way, way back and swung with all my very might.

"Arrrrrrrrrrrrrrrrrrrrrrrgh!" I loudly yelled. "That really, really hurt."

See? Add to this a reminiscence:

It reminded me of Christmas when I was 8 years old and Santa brought me my very, very first toolbox and I was really happy and I took out the hammer.

After you describe how you hit your thumb when you were 8, reach for a quotation from someone else and continue:

I looked at my thumb, and it was pretty, pretty swollen. It reminded me of what that great man James Howell once said: "Pain is the price that God putteth on all things."

Never mind that it didn't really remind you of "what that great man James Howell" once said but rather that you had a *Bartlett's* on the shelf in front of you. Let them think you and James Howell were once on the same bowling team.

The quotation you select doesn't have to be profound or even used in the proper context. All you want it for is to eat up space. If the quotation doesn't have enough words in it, then add filler of your own. Consider:

It reminded me of what that great man James Howell once said: "Pain is the pretty high price God putteth on all things great and small, bright and beautiful, even unto the oblong."

Just don't try this trick with a quotation that is too familiar. I once received several incensed letters from readers after I wrote an Independence Day column that ended:

And so, as we pause in solemn reflection upon the pretty big sacrifices of those who have really gone before us, let us not forget the very, very brave patriot Nathan Hale, who said from the scaffold (where he was about to be hanged), "I really, really regret that I have but one little, tiny life to give for my country. It reminds me of the Christmas when I was 8 and we were playing Hangman.

"Arrrrrrrrrrrrrrrrrrrrrrrrgh!"

There are some pretty, pretty smart readers out there who caught that one right away.

Looking back over what I have written, I've just realized that I have pulled the ultimate columnist's coup. I didn't even have a subject to write about and yet I really, really was able to stretch a feeble pretext for writing into a whole column. It reminds me of what a great man named James Howell once said: "He maketh chicken salad from chicken droppings."

No, I take that back. It reminds me of what Randy Quaid said in the film *Vacation* (which I was watching at the time): "I don't know why they call this stuff Hamburger Helper. I think it's fine by itself."

C.B.

March 8, 1991

Clarence Bernard "C.B." Griffin was possessed of enough love of both baseball and irony that he likely would have been the first to note that had his funeral, on Wednesday, been a double-header, it would have been called on account of rain..

If I try, I can almost hear him loose a bittersweet chuckle at such a thought.

He made it to 78 before the body that once sent hanging curveballs from Central High's home plate to Broad Street's westbound lanes gave out on him.

C.B. and a right-handed hurler named Bob Kline took Central to the state championship in 1929. Kline went on to the majors, where everyone was white. C.B. went on to the league where only the ball was.

The black Columbus Bluebirds of the Negro National League played their home games at Neil Park on those dates when the white Columbus Redbirds were on the road.

C.B. learned early to guess crowd attendance from his perch in center field. The compensation for his play was tethered to their paid-admission fidelity. He took home $4-$5 most days, $22 on the best, 80 cents on the worst. The latter pittance was counted out in pocket change to him during the summer in which his high school teammate Kline -- whose ERA was close to 5.0 -- was being swapped in a midseason trade from the Boston Red Sox to the Philadelphia Athletics that saw $125,000 change hands. At the time, C.B. posted a batting average well beyond .300 against pitchers the likes of 18-year-old right-hander Leroy "Satchel" Paige.

"At the time I faced Satchel," C.B. once conceded with a grimace of respect, "his fastball was his power. He was not a pitcher; he was a thrower. In those days he was raw. He had a power you respected."

He respected, as well, the bat of the Pittsburgh Crawford's Josh Gibson, a player dubbed "the black Babe Ruth." Truth be known, some who saw Gibson bat believed -- out of respect for talent -- it should have been Babe Ruth known as the "white Josh Gibson."

Road games were tough on players such as Griffin. The bologna and bread C.B. bought at rural groceries between Columbus and Chicago, Pittsburgh, Nashville or Kansas City was never covered by a league meal allowance. His hotel was the Pierce-Arrow in which he slept en route to those cities.

In towns that barred him from their hotel rooms and restaurants, he continued to play the game deemed "all American."

A fiscal trampoline, the Negro National League bounced C.B. around from the Bluebirds to the Cleveland Red Sox to the Brooklyn Eagles. He ended his career with the last, playing his final game at Ebbets Field in 1935.

After baseball, C.B. went to work for the Pennsylvania Railroad only to find, when World War II broke out, that his nation was less selective than his National Pastime. He carried an M-1 at the behest of the country reluctant to permit him to shoulder a baseball bat.

When it was over, he was mustered out in time to see Jackie Robinson cross the color line and become baseball's first black star. Though, most certainly, he harbored no bitterness toward Robinson, he could not help but wonder how his life might have been different had he been born in coincidence with his country's late-blooming recognition of its founding principles.

"Do you ever think about that?" he was once asked by a seatmate at a Columbus Clippers game as he rose to leave after the last out at Franklin County Stadium.

"Every day," he admitted, looking off beyond the outfield fence toward Calvary Cemetery's field of dreams. "Every day."

He who could once bat the ball a country mile now sleeps beneath the grave grass in the soldier's section of Calvary Cemetery.

They say it is kept close-trimmed.

"A hitter's field," C.B. would have smiled in wry recognition of all the ones he was forbidden to occupy.

The Sawdust Trail

August 29, 1993

LANCASTER, Ohio - Halfway through the second chorus of *Lord, Don't Give Up on Me*, evangelist Don Green's amplifier did just that.

As if suddenly seized by the Prince of Darkness, the fickle black sound box issued a banshee wail strong enough to drop birds in flight.

Standing atop a hay wagon pressed into service as an altar, soloist Lorna Stiffler, Green's daughter, flinched at the squeal and turned a troubled eye toward her father.

"The devil gets into those things," he apologized to the sparse clutch of believers assembled beneath the canvas shroud he had spread hard by the edge of the intersection of Rts. 22 and 37.

With amused resignation, he assured the faithful: "About the time the service lets out, it will start working just fine."

Green's wife, June, apple-doll smile and swim-goggle spectacles all but hidden behind the organ's music rack, plunged gamely onward into the hymn, as a revival assistant fidgeted with the knobs and switches of the offending amp.

"How many's here to worship Jesus tonight?" Green invited, hoisting a work-hardened paw toward a spot high in the orange-and-dust canvas where the main pole speared through an eyelet and into the windless August swelter.

If Green had a dime for every time he has hammered stakes, cinched guy ropes and raised the main poles for sandlot tabernacles, he wouldn't have to pass the plastic offertory bucket.

"It's just a place where God has chosen to meet us," he said.

Green had a church once, not far from where he had pitched his tent. Several years ago, he and his flock were in the process of rebuilding it when a summer storm hit.

"Lord, you can't let that church go down," he recalled pleading, with nothing separating him from his maker but the newly rigged rafters groaning in the high wind and rain.

"I'm going up there," he told his wife, thinking he could anchor them.

She stopped him just before the collapsing beams knocked out the side walls and left him with a stack of uninsured kindling and a consoling voice he'd known since he first answered the altar call: "There's another place you're going to."

He got over it. When you've spent more time on your knees than a carpet layer, you stop wondering why God's will sometimes plays out like Murphy's law.

Green, aided Wednesday by assistant Harold Glover, has been working the tent since the storm took his church.

He allowed that it is a skin-of-the-teeth operation, and, of the droves of lost souls who didn't fill his folding chairs, he explained, "They're denying the blood. The Bible told us that in the last days this would happen."

Two dozen worshipers, filled with earnest fervor and eager testimony about vanished goiters, craned to hear a volunteer soloist battle the sound of passing truck traffic and sing, "When he said, 'It is finished,' that was just the beginning for me."

"There is someone who needs to come up tonight," Green said, sweeping an arm in the direction of the altar. "This may be the last chance."

His voice had dropped its strident edge and mellowed to a benign resonance, which reached around the room for a worshiper he was certain needed to "pray through" a tribulation.

Fourteen-year-old Curtis Holbrook stepped awkwardly forward and dropped to one knee. Those assembled formed a tight circle around him, like cattle making a wall of warm flesh to buffer a winter calf from a chill that might otherwise claim it.

Curtis' mother, Cindy, draped an arm over his shoulder, her face only inches from a bright tapestry of a beatific Christ robed in crimson and teal.

"God told me to put this tent up," Green said when folks drifted back to their folding chairs. "It's not the best, but I don't ask you for the best, Lord."

Long before there was a Billy Sunday or Graham, tent evangelists were chasing warm weather and unsaved souls, throwing out the figurative lifeline and the literal guy ropes to hoist canvas heavenward.

In the old days, they called it the sawdust trail – for the blanket of wood shavings spread under the tent to keep the grass down and form a cushion to catch those "slain" in the spirit, as surrender, redemption or something in between buckled their knees in the name of the Lord.

Out on the highway Wednesday night, the big trucks rolled out of Lancaster. Their insistent and cadenced straining had provided an evening-long diesel chorus, as believers sang, "Some bright morning when this life is over, I'll fly away."

The service was winding down. "I'm not going to keep you too late tonight," Green promised the lean throng.

Yet the people lingered, even after the benediction, under tent lights beneath which insects cut lazy, halfhearted loops and flourishes.

Flush with the energy of his rededication and looking for something with which to busy himself, Curtis Holbrook made his way around the tent, loosing the ropes that tethered the canvas walls.

If he reckoned the evening's ledger, Green might count one rededication, five testimonials, four healings and a handful of $1 bills.

"If I was in this for the money, I wouldn't have lasted very long," he said with a half-smile, leaving unspoken the terms of whatever private arrangement he had long ago hammered out with his God when he answered the call.

Russian Souvenir

December 18, 1992

MOSCOW – The three boys huddled against the windblown snow whipping across the Moscow River bridge spotted me 50 yards away and moved in for the kill.

Lean and street-wise, they pulled their black-market wares from knapsacks and began pidgin-English spiels before I had a chance to open my mouth. One had matreoshka dolls; another offered a book of Russian commemorative postage stamps. The last displayed a handsome Soviet military badge of the sort typically worn on the lapel of a greatcoat.

"Five dollars," the third one said, cradling the polished metal insignia in his palm.

"Three," I offered, betting that the wind chill factor had tipped haggling in favor of the buyer.

He grimaced in disgust but accepted.

My purchase had the look of authenticity, but with all the knockoffs being foisted upon Red Square tourists I realized that it might well be a cereal-box trinket. But, at $3, I had no right to complain.

Packing my bags for home, I studied the medal. A glistening star whose ruby center showcased a hammer and sickle, it would – if nothing else – serve as a nice conversation piece back in the States. I tossed it in the suitcase.

The customs agent at Moscow's Sheremetyevo 2 Airport greeted me with a cryptic frown when I pushed my luggage into the maw of his X-ray scanner. I couldn't decide whether he was bored, burned out or merely hung over.

He sighed and motioned for me to place my suitcase on the inspection table behind him.

Rifling my packed clothing, he thrust a hand into a suit pocket and pulled out a stack of 50-cent White Castle gift certificates, a present from an old friend who wanted to make sure I never went hungry while on the road. I had forgotten they were in the pocket.

The customs agent pondered them with a smug satisfaction, as if he had discovered a cache of hidden currency. I know that they are worth much more than the ruble, but I couldn't think of how to convince him that they are not actually money. The Russians don't have a word for "slider."

Eventually, losing interest in the certificates, he slid a hand beneath a pile of my dirty laundry and pulled out the military badge.

Obviously he had seen it on the scanner, for he searched only one corner of my suitcase.

He signaled for is superior, a woman who wore the same scowl she had exhibited when she lost the women's shot-put competition in the '68 Olympics.

She grunted and tossed her head toward an office. I took it that she wanted me follow.

Entering a cramped room, she sat down at a desk and began to fill out a customs form, pausing now and then to inspect the smuggled military badge, which, though I had no idea, is the insignia (and property) of a prestigious Russian army division.

"Is there something wrong?" I asked foolishly through the metal grillwork that separated the two of us.

"Don't speak!" she shot back, removing a hand-rolled cigarette from the corner of her mouth and placing it on the edge of the file cabinet.

I had begun to sweat. There swam before me the vision of a gulag in the Siberian tundra. I was wearily bludgeoning boulders with a 9-pound hammer, to the somber accompaniment of *Volga Boatman*.

"Sign," she commanded, stabbing a finger at the customs form.

I did, with a trembling, near-illegible scribble.

She motioned me back to the agent who had discovered the badge. He returned my passport and signaled me to move on.

They kept the badge. I kept a receipt advising me that, anytime I want to return to Russia for a visit during the next three years, I may.

Not on your life.

Michael's Story

May 29, 1992

He tells me he is crafting a wooden box to encase the cremated remains of his boy. He tells me that it consoles him to know that Michael's donated organs are sustaining the lives of several others.

But he does not care to meet tragedy's beneficiaries. It is hard enough to tend the ashes. Another family's loved ones will have to watch the phoenix soar.

Michael Toops died in February. He was 16. A friend and schoolmate was fooling around with a .38.

"He is a good kid," Michael's father, Jack, said of the young man who held the gun that took his son's life by accident. " It was just a bad mistake."

He acknowledged to me, "I don't cry as much as I used to, but I still get the blues."

He returned home from his welder's job at Buckeye Steel one day not long after Michael's death to find a letter from Lifeline of Ohio Organ Procurement, the agency responsible for saving from Michael that which could save other lives.

A gracious and heartfelt missive of thanks, it nonetheless reminded him of the tribute exacted to earn the gratitude of strangers.

"The right lung went into a 48-year-old female from South Dakota – married with one child," Jack said, scanning the letter. According to hospital reports, she was up and walking the corridors not long after the surgery. She hopes to be discharged soon.

The left lung went to a 53-year-old California man. The left kidney and pancreas were transplanted into a 31-year-old central Ohio woman with diabetes and renal disease. The letter indicated that she no longer needs insulin or kidney dialysis.

A lumberyard worker got the right kidney.

"His hobbies are fishing and bowling, and he looks forward to returning to work," Jack read from the letter.

The liver went to a middle-aged man, the heart valves to children awaiting replacements.

After the memorial service, Jack and his wife, Sharon, decided to go ahead with the week they had planned, before Michael's death, at Cape Hatteras, N.C.

"We took a week down there, and we cried on the beach," Jack said. He carried with him a favorite picture of Michael he had taken on the beach at Ocracoke Island, just south of Hatteras on North Carolina's Outer Banks.

He snapped the picture while Michael, unaware, stood with his back to him at tidemark.

"His reflection is in the sand," Jack said, " but it is almost like he's not there."

Of the box he is building for Michael's remains, Jack explained, "We decided to keep Mike's ashes until me or Sharon died, and then sooner or later we will be together."

The collected ashes will be sprinkled in the surf off the shore where Jack took the picture of his son.

He doesn't want to know the faces of those who live on because Michael died. Yet it isn't denial. He has taken the first steps through the heartbreak.

"Before I go to bed every night," Jack said, "I go out into the back yard and talk to Michael. I walk out, and I pick out a star, and I say, 'Hello, Michael.' I tell him how the day went. I tell him not to forget me."

Michael had survived the vicissitudes of chemical dependency and was making great strides toward recovery at the time he was shot.

Flowers were planted in his name at the treatment center where he took his first halting steps away from bad habits. A plaque will honor the brave fight he waged.

"It is a double-edged thing," Jack told me. "There was no reason for his dying, but somebody got a second chance. I wish them well, but I would never want to meet the people who got his organs. I would be looking at part of him. That's my boy."

So he talks to the stars.

Have a Friend for Lunch

April 11, 1993

For those of you who endured the TV commercials featuring beef-industry pitchman James Garner, this is a column about the "other" red meat: us.

Humans. Homo sapiens.

As is the tradition each April, the memory of the infamous Colorado prospector Alferd (yep-that's-how-he-spelled-it) Packer is about to be honored again by students at the University of Colorado.

Those aware that students at Boulder have never canceled a party for want of a reason might think this Packer thing a frivolous excuse to drink cheap beer. They are only partly right.

This year marks the silver anniversary of Alferd Packer Day. It is a special time at the student union eatery, the Alferd Packer Grill.

Contests will abound to see who can eat the most raw onions, Rocky Mountain oysters, ribs, beef tartare, pizza and hot peppers.

All of this will be followed, appropriately enough, by a belch-off (winner selected by loudest applause)

Why celebrate Packer? Who knows? Why did folks laugh at Jeffrey Dahmer jokes?

To the credit of Colorado students, they at least waited until almost a century after the trial to yuk it up about cannibalism.

Yet despite that passage of time, historians are still trying to seine fact from legend and apocrypha in the case of Alferd Packer.

Drifter, gold prospector, petty thief, Packer trekked into the San Juan Mountains with five companions in 1874.

Steve Knutson, who manages restaurant operations for the University of Colorado, appraises of Packer's survival of that star-crossed expedition, "He was the only one who came out fat and sassy at the end of winter."

Packer, who allowed to authorities that he, indeed, had killed in self-defense one crazed companion who had come at him with a hatchet, denied charges of cannibalism.

He was convicted of murdering all five.

Although the story probably is no more than Packer lore, Judge M.B. Gerry is said to have invoked at Alferd's sentencing, "There were seven Democrats in Hinsdale County, but you, you voracious, man-eating SOB, you ate five of them. I sentence you to be hanged by the neck until you are dead, dead, dead, as a warning against reducing the Democratic population of the state."

Spared the noose and granted an appeal on a technicality, Packer was again tried. Found guilty of involuntary manslaughter, he was sent to prison.

A campaign by a Colorado newspaper to win parole for Packer led to his freedom in 1901.

He died six years later.

Five years ago, a handful of forensic pathologists traveled to the mass grave of Packer's victims near Lake City, Colo., to exhume and examine the remains.

The leader, a flamboyant professor of law and forensic science named James Starrs, dispensed his findings to the press -- so one account contends -- while wearing a T-shirt emblazoned "Gimme Five! The Packer Project," claiming that Packer was guilty as sin.

The "de-fleshing" marks on too many of the bones made it impossible to dismiss cannibalism. Also, four of the five victims had died of hatchet blows to the head.

Sounds like a good enough reason to party at Boulder.

This being the 25th anniversary of Alferd Packer Day, students have commissioned a T-shirt embossed with previous years' winners of the annual T-shirt slogan contest. The top slogans, from best to worst, or vice versa:

- Eat them up. Eat them raw, raw, raw!
- You're not just frying; you're frying the friendly guys.
- Nothin' spells lovin' like someone in the oven.
- When you care enough to eat the very best.
- A kinder, tastier nation.
- You've bit the raw one, baby (uh-huh).
- Finger lickin' good.
- If you can't beat'em, eat'em.
- Have a friend for lunch today.
- The original party cannibal.

Ah, yes. One can almost imagine old Alferd out in the wilds with the fellas, anticipating the evening's repast sizzling on a makeshift spit, admiring a Colorado moon rising over a San Juan peak and toasting, "Boys, it just doesn't get any better than this."

The Drifter

October 5, 1992

The world said goodbye to Ronald Adkins with a terse journalistic farewell: "Sheriff's reports say he was a drifter who had been in the local veterans hospital."

He had a pocket full of Veterans Administration Librium and all that he owned in life packed into a duffel bag three weeks ago when he stepped in front of a car on Rt.35 near Chillicothe and ended his 47 years of life.

Some say it was an accident. Some say Adkins, a veteran of two tours of Vietnam, snuffed the candle by his own hand.

The news of his death reached Bernie Pontones, local president of Vietnam Veterans of America, hardly in time for him to make the graveside services.

"I ran down to Ronnie's funeral," Pontones said. "By the time I had worked my way through road construction to the funeral home, they were gone."

He hurried out to Bethel Methodist Church, outside Chillicothe. But when he arrived the mourners had gone, and a grave crew of three was in the process of putting Adkins into the ground.

"It was full military honors," Adkins' brother, Ray, recalled of the services. "The flag and the casket...Rifle salute, taps."

Ray was in high school when his brother went off with the Green Berets to fight in Vietnam.

"He would never talk about it," Ray said. "I remember seeing the news stories. It didn't make a whole lot of sense to me, either."

Ron Adkins returned from Vietnam, married, settled in Texas and went to work as a welder.

Ray saw him infrequently and likely saw less the shadows of any ghosts his brother probably battled.

Ron moved around a lot and was no stranger to VA hospitals.

Said Ray, "They'd keep him a few days, give him pills, then let him out."

Pontones lamented, "I don't know what the VA did. I don't know what the VA is doing, and it is just one more guy down the tubes.

"Here is a man who did so much for his country and yet was completely alienated. How can no one reach out to a man like that and permit him to drift into a sort of nether world within his own country?"

Some time ago, Pontones went prowling into the archives of the state of Ohio to learn what had happened to returning Vietnam veterans. Locking in on state death certificates for one year (1975) he found 1 percent of the dead were Vietnam-era veterans.

"Roughly 20 percent were suicides," Pontones pointed out. "Twenty percent were homicides. Twenty percent were various cancers (remember Agent Orange). Twenty percent were automobile accidents, most of which were single-vehicle accidents."

Ray Adkins said of the investigation after his brother's death, "It was dismissed as though, oh well, there is another one."

Another what?

In this year of political campaigns, there is no shortage of those willing to lavish upon this country's veterans all manner of praise and purple bombast.

None of that will do much for Ron Adkins.

"Some people could leave it over there and go on," Ray told me. "Some couldn't."

For a long time, as Bernie Pontones would freely admit, the curse of the Vietnam veteran has been that he has been unjustly stereotyped as a baby-killing sociopath who returned to the United States only to unleash his unvented rage upon, for instance, the unsuspecting lunchtime diner of some fast-food palace.

In truth, more suffer the quiet indignity and lonesome deaths such as Ron Adkins'.

The names of the dead of Vietnam are not inscribed exclusively upon the black marble of the wall in Washington, D.C. Far more, as we approach the day that honors their sacrifice, survived the battle only to succumb to the lingering effects of its memory.

This country was only too good at teaching Ron Adkins how important it was for him to be willing to die for it in Vietnam. When he died, instead, in Chillicothe, they called him a drifter.

The Church Baptism

July 24, 1993

KASKASKIA, Ill. – The first problem confronting the seven men who waded into the floodwater rising inside the Church of the Immaculate Conception – to rescue what they could – was the quartet of Black Angus steer that huddled like chubby, sloe-eyed altar boys between the communion rail and the sacristy.

The cattle had somehow wandered into the empty church after the Kaskaskia levee broke, while island residents were being ferried to the safety of nearby St. Mary, Mo.

Frightened and wary, they moved off to the side as Randolph County Sheriff Ben Picou, a boyhood member of the church, led rescuers to the altar.

Behind him, in the sanctuary, massive wooden pews – like barges cut adrift – floated about, banging into the walls of the old church that was first established when Kaskaskia was yet a French colony in the Louisiana Territory.

In a building next door, and safely set in concrete, rested the original church bell. It had long ago been hauled up the Mississippi by pole barge and presented to the frontier faithful as a gift from the king of France.

As the water in the church rose, Picou and his comrades began carrying statuary, holy water fonts, vestments, flags and crucifixes up to the safety of the choir bay.

The altar posed a major problem. Too ponderous and unwiedly to be wrestled up the narrow stairway, there seemed no way to rescue it until Picou decided that with enough muscle and rope it might be hoisted from the sanctuary to the bay.

There was plenty of muscle, but no rope in sight.

"Cut down the belfry ropes," Picou ordered. A volunteer scrambled up a precariously narrow, two-story catwalk and sliced off two ropes near the base of the steeple.

Floating free in the water, the altar was pushed into position. The crucifix toppled from its crown just before the hoist ropes were cinched.

Attended by much grunting and hauling, the altar slowly made it up over the lip of the choir bay rail, dripping water all the way.

Below, in the sanctuary, the confessional had broken free and was listing to the side like a mystical, gothic ocean liner with its forecastle and bridge peeping above water, now chest high and still creeping up.

"We used to fight over who would carry these censers," Picou laughed as he studied a pair of chained incense burners and remembered his days as an altar boy.

"I noticed you saved everything but the confessional," one of the volunteers chided him. "Too many bad memories, huh?"

The choir bay was jammed to overflowing with trappings of the faith. No room remained for a pair of communion rails.

Down in the murky water, an uprooted garter snake slithered among the pews. A copy of *Father McGuire's Easy Elementary Catechism* floated by, a frog squatting atop it.

There was not much left to do but save the steer.

Spooked cattle, with their heads barely above water, do not suffer lightly the tugging and hauling of novice cowboys.

Thrashing, they were pushed outside and lassoed to the sides of rescue boats.

Great black eyes rolled back in their heads. They flailed hoofs against the boat as the outboards chugged to life and slowly began moving them to the nearest high ground, about 2,000 yards away.

"Keep their noses out of the water," Picou ordered, cradling the thick neck of one of the beasts as boats drew near the embankment of the levee.

Freed from their ropes, they scampered up in to the grass and began munching lazily as though the ordeal had been a bad dream from which they had just happily shaken themselves awake.

The boats pulled away. Far off in the distance, the tiny orange sliver of a Coast Guard skiff could be seen tied to the front door of the Church of the Immaculate Conception.

Picou's band had saved what they could. Perhaps only the cradle Catholics among the group understood why it was so important to hazard such peril to rescue articles of the faith that – save for a handful of irreplaceable exceptions – could have been replenished from a religious supply store. But maybe for a few hours, it kept some of the volunteers' minds off their displaced friends and kin, ruined crops and drowned livestock.

"I wish I had a picture of me with my arm around that steer's neck," Picou mused as the boats nosed toward the landing for the ferry. A slow smile crept up the corners of his mouth.

"I could have used that come election."

St. Paul Shaver

July 10, 1992

Tony Hopson watched the white hearse, untrailed by mourners' cars, ease slowly into Evergreen Cemetery. Climbing off the mower, he nodded to fellow groundskeeper Bobby Turner and said, "I guess we have to be pallbearers."

In death, as in life, Paul Shaver, "the Bishop of High Street," was counting on the kindness of strangers to get him where he needed to go.

Jim Triplett, Shaver's landlord for more than a dozen years, arrived at the cemetery a few minutes after the hearse. In one hand he held a slim book, titled *Difficult Funerals*. His free hand he lent to the business of unloading the cloth-covered casket.

"He had wanted to go back to Tennessee," Triplett said, after he and the others had rested their burden on the belts that held it suspended above the yawning grave. " He wanted to go back home and start something he was going to call the Tabernacle of God."

Even as he lay dying of cancer in the VA hospital in Dayton, the 74-year-old street preacher railed that God was going to spare his life for the thankless mission of rescuing the unsaved in Knoxville.

For more than 20 years, Bible in one hand, a tambourine and a crude pine cross in the other, Shaver spent six days a week proselytizing Downtown Columbus shoppers as they passed between the grits-and-gravel rasp of his sidewalk exhortations and the lunch special at Woolworth.

I bought him breakfast one brutal winter morning several years ago. He thanked me by threatening, "Any word you say against me will take you to hell! I'm St. Paul Shaver, the high priest of God."

He already had decided that journalists belong in that mixed bag of hopeless pagans that includes – according to him – adulterers, cross-dressers, Presbyterians, luke-warm Baptists, hypocritical priests, Hare Krishnas, Moonies, mimes and Jerry Falwell. All of us are condemned to recall his words above the sound of creaking hot hinges when the gates of hell open to welcome us to our eternal reward.

On more than one occasion he was hauled into court when his ministry stepped over the line that separates the rights of free speech and the laws that define public nuisance. Twice he was carted off to mental institutions, only to be released by confounded doctors who were no match for an evangelical fervor neither reason nor Thorazine could subdue.

Someone once asked why it is that when we talk to God, it is praying, but when God talks to us, it is schizophrenia.

God talked to him, St. Paul Shaver confided to me seven years ago. He appeared before him, Shaver said, in the one-room apartment that he called home on W. Main Street. God placed a jeweled crown on the head of the Bishop of High Street and told him he had work for him to do in Knoxville. God promised a school bus to transport his ministry south.

There would be no fewer sinners than in Columbus, but the winters might be kinder.

Triplett, standing at the head of the casket, softly intoned, "And I heard a great voice from heaven saying, 'Behold, the Tabernacle of God is with men.'"

Mortician Jim Shields, his outstretched palm cradling four clods of grave dirt, continued, "We commit his soul to God and his ashes to the earth."

His fingers closed around the soil, and a fine powder sprinkled upon the casket lid. Wearily, he added, "Ashes to ashes, dust to dust. Lord have mercy. Amen."

When Shaver became eligible for Social Security several years ago, his landlord urged him to take his entitlement for all the years he had worked as a short-order cook before being called to his do-it-yourself ministry. But Shaver would have none of Uncle Sam's mammon. He continued paying his rent in the $1 bills and loose change that strangers dropped in his tambourine, continued to thrive on a diet of eggs and religion, both hard-boiled.

On a July afternoon whose passing seconds were measured by the eerie clicking of gears that lower casket to grave vault, St. Paul Shaver likely would have preferred to be back at his perch in front of Woolworth, chastening "brazing hussies" for wearing too much lipstick or too little skirt.

But unburdened at last of his calling, at rest between flanking hemlock and maple – the spot marked by flowers purloined from a nearby grave – he finally got to have a ground-breaking for his Tabernacle of God.

The Little Red Sports Car

September 18, 1991

If I were to place a personal ad for myself, it would read something like this:

Regular guy, medium build, so-so looks, average intelligence, seeks same in a companion for predictable evenings listening to middle-of-the-road music and eating American cheese on white bread.

What can I say? I'm ordinary. When a fast-food clerk inquires, "Hot sauce or mild?" I always ask whether there's anything in between. I've never been white-water rafting and never owned a tarantula, and most of my dogs have been nondescript brown. People who say they never forget a face are generally willing to make an exception in my case.

Salespeople have a form of radar that detects mediocrity right off the bat. In a men's store, the "sales associates" seem to know immediately that the only thing I own that is monogrammed is my bowling ball. The clerk dispatched to help me usually wears beltless, double-knit slacks and standard-issue mailman's shoes.

So it was, when the time arrived to trade in my old beige car a few weeks ago, that I felt fairly confident I would buy something sensible, something an insurance actuary might drive.

Other people drive cars with names such as Cougar and Firebird. I drive cars with names like Plymouth Reliant, Dodge Functional, Ford Average.

The only vehicle I had decided in advance not to test-drive was the Chevrolet Caprice Classic. Police departments seem to be crazy about them, but to me they resemble Latvia's attempt to crack the U.S. car market.

At the car dealership, I surrendered my keys to the used-car appraiser and headed straight for a bland, blue, four-door sedan. All the radio presets were keyed to the station I hear when the hygienist measures the gum pockets around my incisors. I was about to ask whether they had the same model in beige when I saw the little red sports car.

It was low and sleek and sexy. It had aluminum alloy wheels, fuel injection, chrome exhausts, a sunroof and, yes, the same price range as the first house I owned. It was not merely red. It was the red that fire departments use for hook and ladders and Frederick's uses for bras. The interior was black on black.

"Nah," I said to myself. "If I take that car home, Debra will hire a private investigator tomorrow. First three warning signs of an affair: (1) lipstick on collar, (2) hang-up calls, (3) new red car with chrome exhausts.

A fellow with whom I work bought a red sports coupe a few weeks ago only to have a female friend sniff, "Oh, the midlife crisis color."

I saw a statistic somewhere suggesting that police are much more likely to stop a red car than one that is, say, bland blue. And why would I want all that horsepower when my style of driving mirrors the timidity of porcupine foreplay?

The sensible sedan was called an Accord. That's just the kind of name I've always bought. Sounds like a non-aggression pact between Afghanistan and Sri Lanka. The sporty model was called a Prelude. That name has a vaguely carnal ring to it, as if Prelude were not a car but an ointment you take along on your honeymoon.

I test-drove the sedan. It was roomy, conservatively styled and, like every other thing I've ever bought in my life, utterly practical.

I bought the red sports coupe.

I drive with the sunroof open and the radio cranked up. I'm thinking about getting one of those bumper stickers whose message taunts, "If it's too loud, you're too old."

There is a bit more muscle to the car than I'm accustomed to flexing.

You don't need a chain saw if all you're doing is carving a turkey. It wants to go 70. I want to go 55.

"Nice car," longtime acquaintances admire with the incredulity they might demonstrate if I had my nose pierced. "You having an affair?"

The Cruelest Death There Is

February 19, 1993

FRAZEYSBURG, Ohio – The windshield vista that greets a city traveler approaching the Muskingum County hamlet of Frazeysburg suggests a plain-spoken honesty about the town's major virtues and minor vices.

Roadside signs touting the 4-H chapter and Aunt B's Country Kitchen conjure up a Mayberry wholesomeness. Barn sides advertising Mail Pouch tobacco acknowledge forgivable sins.

Not unlike a hundred other rural villages that freckle the landscape of eastern Ohio, Frazeysburg possesses a pastoral homeliness that, at once, makes it inviting to those inclined to sit and visit a spell, and forgettable to those with more pressing business on the other side of the hill.

A town such as Frazeysburg gets good after a while at handling life's commerce – big and small – remembering first names and conducting last rites.

Country modesty, one suspects, tempers the urge toward public gloating over personal good fortune in Frazeysburg. But bad news rides a swift mount.

It didn't take long for word to get around Sunday that the life of 5-year-old Sara West had been snuffed during the night in a slaying as barbarous as it was diabolic.

The child, though killed in nearby Zanesville, had kin in Frazeysburg. Her grandmother and great-grandmother live there. Sara's mother, Tracy, grew up close by in Nashport.

The particulars of the mutilation slaying – to which a 16-year-old baby sitter has confessed – are so ugly that one can only hope, for the sake of the child's suffering, that the bullet spared her a consciousness of the grim work of the hunting knife.

It is as difficult for Frazeysburg to look at Sara's photograph and not ask "Why?" as it is for the town to learn the history of the boy who confessed, Billy Joe Shaeffer, and not ask "How?"

How could a 16-year-old, whose publicly acknowledged heroes (Jeffrey Dahmer and Charles Manson) claimed two dozen victims, not speak of his twin idols without sounding a fire bell to some listener, somewhere?

How could his family listen to him give breath to his yearning to kill someone, "just to see what it was like," without hearing the ominous ticking that inched clock hands toward calamity?

Shaeffer apparently had raised enough eyebrows to draw the attention, variously, of Zanesville school and court officials, mental health and children's services workers.

But the attention was insufficient to prevent what happened to Sara West, sometime between the Saturday late news and last call, in a white frame house on Zanesville's bleak and hilly Ridge Road.

While the court wrestled with the issue of whether Shaeffer ought to be tried as an adult, and while armchair shrinks pondered the meaning of the scribbled satanic symbols on the boy's school notebooks, Frazeysburg picked up the sad task of seeing Sara to her rest.

To Carl and Carolyn Vencil, who run the town's funeral home, fell the hard business of restoring a hideously mutilated child to an appearance that would suggest nothing so much as peaceful slumber.

"You can't prepare yourself for it," Carl said, shaking his head. "The death of a child has to be the cruelest death there is. Nothing you could say to the parents is going to make them feel any better."

He pondered the small navy dress spangled with roses, the mauve sash and the lace jabot, a tiny rose at the throat. It might seem enchanting if purchased for a piano recital.

Up the road at the cemetery, township Trustee Rick Priest paced off eight footsteps in the fresh snow from the headstone of Sara's great-grandfather and faced right.

"Right here," he said, nodding to the gravedigger.

On the other side of the fence from the child's grave, the brown stubble of last year's corn harvest peeked through the mantle of snow. The corn will be up once more before grass again flourishes on the ground broken to receive Sara West.

The fever-dream madness of her killing is too much for Frazeysburg. Townsfolk in such places can offer the family only a comforting touch, a generous shoulder, a prayer, a pot roast, a pie.

But from such simple and tender mercies does healing send forth its first, tentative roots.

Forever England

August 14, 1991

OCRACOKE, ISLAND, N.C. – A noontime deluge had made a two-lane canal of the road leading back to the cemetery in Ocracoke village. To the west and the Carolina mainland, thunderheads the hue of African violets threatened another onslaught. Though raindrops spotted the plastic cover sheathing a letter posted near four British graves, the missive was still quite legible:

"U.S. Coast Guard Station Ocracoke deeply regrets it can no longer fly the sovereign ensign of the United Kingdom over the brave sailors who gave their lives while fighting for freedom and to protect the U.S. coast during World War II.

"There are those who have no scruples or morals and desecrate this sacred place of honor. They keep stealing the British national ensign time and time again. I truly hope that those of you who respect and care for this small part of England as much as the men of Station Ocracoke will understand."

The letter was signed by Chief Boatswain Mate Peter Stone, the commander of the U.S. Coast Guard Station at Ocracoke.

Above the posted letter a white flagpole bare of any flag stood sentry over a quartet of headstones marking the graves of Lt. Thomas Cunningham, telegraph operator Stanley Craig and two unknowns who were part of the crew of the *HMS Bedfordshire.*

The *Bedfordshire* had been sent by England to the waters off the Carolina Outerbanks in the spring of 1942. She was a converted fishing trawler. 170 feet long and outfitted with deck guns and depth charges for stalking German U-boats that had been picking off traffic in the Atlantic shipping lanes like fish in a barrel.

Manned by four officers and 33 sailors of the Royal Naval Patrol Service, the *Bedfordshire* began patrolling the waters off the Carolina coast where, in the first four months of 1942, 66 ships had been lost. But hunter became prey in the late night hours of May 11.

The German submarine *U-558* caught the silhouette of the *Bedfordshire* off Cape Lookout and sent her to the bottom in waters grimly nicknamed "The Graveyard of the Atlantic." Not a man survived.

Ocracoke native Ronald O'Neal recalls today that he was hauling sand along the beach with another fellow a few days after the sinking when the two happened upon a body washed up in the surf.

"It was one of the unknowns," O'Neal said.

Three other bodies of *Bedfordshire* crew members were recovered and buried on a plot of land near a family cemetery on Ocracoke.

Over the years, the care of the British cemetery has passed from the townsfolk to the members of the nearby Coast Guard station.

"We take great pride in doing it," Stone allowed. "Out of respect and duty, it is just right that we do it."

Each year on the date of the sinking of the *Bedfordshire*, a service is conducted outside the small picket fence framing four granite markers. The sea breeze is heavy with the crack of salute rifles, a bugler playing *Taps*, a mournful Requiem offered by a lone bagpipe player performing *Amazing Grace*, the hymn of the Royal Naval Patrol Service.

But now there is no flag to salute.

Stone has lost seven of them to vandals since March.

"The last time I put one up with a cable and chain," he said, " and they ripped *it* off."

"It's one of the dirtiest, commonest things I've heard of," spat O'Neal. "Those people were here fighting for our country. It burns me up."

He and Stone have decided that their lone recourse at this point might be to heighten the flag pole and, using a cherry picker, attach a flag to the top of the pole with no halyard to lower or raise it.

That reverence and tribute have come to require such extreme measures is a pity that burns as a slow rage in Stone and O'Neal and mocks the words of British poet Rupert Brooke engraved on a brass plate near the headstones.

If I should die, think only this of me:
That there's some corner of a foreign field
That is forever England

The Mother of My Children

December 11, 1991

A shared love and a medical necessity throw us together on a chaotic Monday morning. Our 17-year-old Annie has begun the week with a nasty cough and a fever that frightens both of us.

Operational necessity dictates that we split nursing duties. Suzanne volunteers to chauffeur Annie to the doctor. I will make the pharmacy run and the chicken soup.

In the doctor's office, Annie clutches her mother's hand and leans on her shoulder. She thinks she might faint. She feels as if she is dying. The relentless bark of the cough ceases only when she loses the breath to do it.

Acute bronchitis, the doctor pronounces upon inspecting the X-ray – nearly pneumonia. It is clear he is weighing the prospect of putting her in the hospital, although he doesn't say as much, He decides to watch it first for 24 hours.

Her mother and I sit at the dining room table sipping coffee, ears trained to the back bedroom, from which the coughing finally gives way to slumber.

"Do you know what today is?" she quizzes me when we are finally able to think of something other than the fever thermometer.

I shake my head.

"Twenty-three years, it would have been," she tells me. "This is our anniversary."

"My God, that's right," I acknowledge. Twenty-three years ago we had pledged "I do" in a Navy chapel outside Washington, D.C.

"Fraternizing with an enlisted man," her superior officers had sniffed when they learned we had been dating. Nothing good could come of it, they warned. The Catholic chaplain seemed twice as skeptical. Not only was I a non-com, I was a non-Catholic as well.

A moment of awkward silence follows my inability to recall the significance of the date. She defuses it with laughter.

There was precious little of that six years ago when it all ended.

"I'll make some Jell-O for her," she tells me. "Doctor wants to get that temperature down."

We were both children of parents who might have divorced – perhaps even should have – but didn't.

How curiously we now look back on our time together.

"Don't you think of those years as wasted?" I have been asked.

"I think children can help you overcome it," I have claimed. They are the proverbial phoenix rising from the nuptial ashes, the treasure you didn't know was hidden in the mattress until you ripped the marriage bed apart.

"I can stay here and keep an eye on her if you have to write a column," Suzanne offers.

"No," I tell her. "You're needed back at work. I'll keep you posted this afternoon. I think once she is able to sleep, and once the antibiotic takes hold, her temperature will come down."

"You know I love you both, don't you?" she asks.

I nod.

Friends of mine have told me about divorced couples who – years after domestic relations court has made final what religion thought permanent – salivate over the possibility of running over their former mate in a parking lot.

It is not hate but apathy that is the opposite of love.

"Tell John I said hello," I tell her as she leaves.

"Tell Debra," she replies.

There is a quiet in the room from which, for several hours, nothing but a nagging hack could be heard.

In our own ways, we try to make peace with our past. Sometimes it takes analysis. Sometimes it simply takes time. Sometimes – as the Bible reminds us – it is a child who leads us.

"Don't forget," Suzanne reminds me, "give her 500 milligrams of the antibiotic at 8 p.m."

"I know," I tell her.

In a room at the end of the hallway there burns a candle that has lighted a friendship I once thought impossible.

Divorce has taught both of us how to act as if we just might have celebrated 23 years together on Dec. 9.

Jurrasic Toots

November 4, 1991

Most readers are likely aware of the long-standing dispute over whether cows contribute to the greenhouse effect by burping methane.

Many readers, as well, may have seen a recent news item indicating that, in their time, dinosaurs may have abetted global warming.

In short, researchers in California theorize that dinosaur flatulence warmed the prehistoric atmosphere. Scientists postulated this after studying fossilized brontosaurus dung.

I'm not sure just how one studies fossilized dinosaur dung. I don't even know how you fit it into the back of the Isuzu for the trip back to the lab.

In any case, that short article piqued my interest. I wanted to learn more.

"What was the typical size or mass of a dinosaur toot?" I inquired of *Dispatch* librarian Jim Hunter. He rolled his eyes, as he often does when I ask questions he considers unique. I wanted to know because, if I can find a reliable answer, I think I have a shot at the Nobel Prize next year by taking the conclusion of the Los Angeles dinosaur researchers one step further.

Humans have wondered for scores of decades just how it was that these giant prehistoric reptiles could rule the Earth for 140 million years, then suddenly become extinct.

Some theorize the Earth's climate cooled during the end of the Cretaceous Period. Others say an exploding nearby star released enough radiation to profoundly change the weather on Earth and that the combined effects of radiation and cold killed the dinosaurs.

Hunter was not long in providing me with an answer, although I'm not sure what the Nobel judges will think of how he reached his conclusion.

By a bit of simple math he concluded that cows produce 3.75 liters of methane a day for each pound they weight. If dinosaurs did the same, one that weighed 70 tons would release 525,000 liters of flatulence a day, enough to fill about 262,000 of those big unbreakable Pepsi bottles, although I don't know why you would want to.

That is a generous contribution to global warming. But I don't care how serious you are about the problem, I can't believe that even the most ardent activist would want to get that close to the tail of a brontosaurus in one of those little Greenpeace rafts.

Compound that methane output by the number of dinosaurs roaming the Earth – billions and billions.

It is probably good that dinosaurs were no smarter. Although you could park a school bus in the stomach of a brontosaurus, his brain was no larger than that of a freshman fraternity brother. With that kind of brain, had dinosaurs discovered opposable thumbs and Bic lighters, they could have welded the Eiffel Tower before breakfast.

So what is this theory that I think will win me the Nobel Prize?

I think dinosaurs made themselves extinct.

There were billions of dinosaurs creating zillions of liters of methane every day. The entire globe was nothing but a huge re-enactment of the campfire scene in *Blazing Saddles*.

There was no place for this hot air to go but up. It rose into the atmosphere and began drifting with air currents toward the polar icecaps. As this heat built up, it caused huge chasms in ice formations. Eventually, glaciers the size of Indiana started sliding around the sides of the globe.

Oblivious to this, the dinosaurs kept eating and tooting. More glaciers broke loose. They rumbled over the dinosaurs, crushing the last of them into extinction 65 million years ago.

It is further my thesis that cows have taken up where dinosaurs left off. The U.S. Department of Agriculture is studying the problem, although I don't know what they think they can do about it.

I would like to win the Nobel Prize. I hear it is a blender or something like that.

Eager to fortify my research, I tracked down our trusty librarian, Hunter.

"What do you want now?" he said, rolling his eyes.

"Could you find out how that 525,000 liters of methane a day would have been altered if there were White Castles during the Jurassic Period?"

A Few Well-read Men

August 14, 1989

News item: U.S. Marine Corps Commandant Gen. A.M. Gray has ordered his troops to start reading literature. He has prepared a recommended list of book titles and is requiring that non-commissioned officers and below read two to four books a year and that officers and higher ranking non-coms read as many as six.

D.I. Fall in, you maggots! Outta those racks! C'mon! C'mon! Spinelli, Douglass, Washington! Front and center, you worms. You guys call yourself Marines? Ha! Carruthers, get off that bunk! You dreaming about your girlfriend back home? Forget her. You were history the day you left for Parris Island. Now line up.

OK, troops. The colonel is coming by for inspection tomorrow. I want you people to be ready. Spinelli, you're first.

Spinelli: Sir

D.I. Don't you dare look me in the eye, you little worm, or I'll choke you down to parade rest!

Spinelli: Sir, I'm sorry, sir.

D.I. You're sorry all right. You're been sorry since the day you arrived. Now, Spinelli, tell me about *Moby Dick*.

Spinelli: Sir, *Moby Dick*, sir, is a story about this old guy with one leg who tried to find the great white, sir.

D.I. Is that all you know?

Spinelli: *(Beginning to break down)* Sir, this one guy lives, but I can't remember his name, sir.

D.I. Drop and give me 50, maggot! Washington? You think this stuff is funny? You tell me about *Moby Dick*.

Washington: Sir, Melville's whale is a metaphor for man's unceasing efforts to search for a meaning to life, sir. Ishmael's voyage has generally been conceded to be a journey of "Faustian self-discovery," sir. By depicting Ahab as a man who, in the end, is destroyed by his obsession, Melville is actually writing a broader critique about the self-destructive enforced moralism of his age.

D.I. Good, Washington. Good. Douglass. Your turn. And you'd better be good because what you do with a pugil stick doesn't mean jack if you don't understand *The Sound and the Fury*.

Douglass: Sir, please, sir. Not Faulkner, sir.

D.I. Maybe you'd prefer instead to enlighten us on Proust's *Remembrance of Things Past*.

Douglass: (Between choked sobs) Sir, no. Not Proust. Please. He never ate a hot dog or kissed a girl or went to the can that he didn't write it down, sir. Sir, it's all like a big Springsteen song that don't rhyme. Please, sir.

D.I. *(Slapping a riding crop against his palm)* There are only two ways to teach worms. I can feed you or I can beat you, and I don't have the money to feed you. And there's only three ways you're gonna leave this island. In a box. In a straightjacket. Or in the uniform of the most literate fighting force in the world. Now, Douglass. Tell me about Faulkner.

Douglass: Sir, I don't know no Faulkner, sir. I joined the Corps because Jiffy Lube fired me for incompetence.

D.I. *(Grabs Douglass by the shirt causing a copy of* Cliff Notes *for* The Sound and the Fury *to slip out from under the waistband of his shorts. A collective sigh rises from the other recruits)* What have we here, Douglass? You think you can learn Faulkner just by picking up some literary companion that talks about the old man's "biblical parallelism" or "Joycean stream of consciousness"?

Douglass: Sir, I just want to kill people, sir, not talk to them about Faulkner.

D.I. That's the problem with all you maggots. You read James Fenimore Cooper and all you see is dead Indians.

Carruthers: Sir, actually I found Cooper's prose to be rather trite and wooden, the characters overstated and the scenes and plot lines so, well, fantastic, sir, that even the dullest clod could see through them, sir.

D.I. *(Nodding appreciatively)* Now there's a Marine. I can put a blindfold on Carruthers and he can disassemble and reassemble Thomas Pynchon's plots in five minutes. OK, enough of this. Line up troops. We got bayonet practice. Carruthers, call the cadence.

Carruthers: I don't know but I been told.

Troops: *(In unison)* I don't know but I been told.

Carruthers: Marlowe wrote what Shakespeare stole.

Troops: Sound off, one, two, three, four.

Pony Girl

February 27, 1989

I lit a fire in the wood stove Sunday and built a parapet of cardboard boxes within an easy toss of the flames.

My pack rat ways had spawned several teetering stacks of boxes in the garage. Having promised to clear them before the first crocus tasted spring, I appraised the precariously leaning heaps with the cold disdain of a grass-green ensign inspecting a muster of drunk recruits fresh back from Cinderella liberty.

I made quick work of the first several boxes, pausing only to refill my coffee cup, but stopped dead when an assortment of old snapshots tumbled from a manila envelope I was about to pitch.

The little girl in cowboy chaps was sitting atop a pony as white as a Christmas moon. A bright kerchief fanned out from her throat. The black hat of a dime store gaucho was cocked behind her blond curls. She smiled at the old photographer who had wandered into our neighborhood one summer leading his pony, a tripod slung over his shoulder as nonchalantly as a hobo's pack.

What was his fee? Two dollars? Three? My mother fetched the bills from her hiding place under the edge of the kitchen linoleum. There was enough for one pony photo of one child, my older sister, Mary. Sulking, I was told my chance would come the next time the pony man returned. He never did.

My sister does not know I have the photograph. Shortly before my grandmother's death a few years ago, she summoned me to her apartment and told me to help myself to her snapshots. In her last days, she had tried to identify all of them. Laboring with dimmed vision and palsied hand she captioned as many as she could. "Mike Harden. When?? Just a kid," she penned on the back of my second-grade photo.

If life were an AT&T commercial I would have snatched up the telephone and called my sister in Illinois the moment I first spied the pony picture. Instead, I decided to send it to her without comment and wait for her reaction.

I don't see much of Mary anymore. She works for a cable TV company in Normal, Ill. Birthday greetings and Christmas cards come laden with the latest school pictures of her three children, snippets of family news, columns she has scissored from her local newspaper.

We come together at wakes and weddings, trying to steal enough time after the vows and eulogies are finished to catch up on our lives. But 35 summers after she posed on horseback, flanked by picket fence and sugar maple, we are still trying to "find the time."

Mary and I were the Singing Hardens, a pre-pubescent, Pentecostal duo constantly cajoled into crooning *Have You Talked To the Man Upstairs?* to a Short North congregation that paid us in "Amens."

My voice changed one year at summer camp precisely between the first and second verses of a talent show performance of *I've Been Working on the Railroad*. Having blown the chance to win a first-place prize of a Camp Mary Orton T-shirt (it went to a child contortionist), I was inconsolable. On the last day of camp I learned that Mary had saved her camp spending money to buy me – you guessed it – a camp T-shirt.

Shy, though ever full of wise and selfless counsel, she took me aside the year I turned 13, looked deep into my eyes and told me I smelled bad. Only Mary could have broached the subject of deodorant use and escaped a split lip.

She took me by the hand again the summer I turned 15. I was moony, pimpled and dateless, though smelling somewhat better than at 13.

"Look," she said, "the reason you don't have any dates is because you wear your heart right out where everyone can see it. You have to keep it a mystery if you want to keep them interested."

I was away in the Navy when she said, "I do." Her letters followed me around the country and across the Pacific, always packed with snapshots, big sister encouragement, good cheer.

I'm 42 now, my sister 43. She still smells better than me, though my voice doesn't crack when I sing *I've Been Working on the Railroad*.

"Who taught time to fly?" K.T. Oslin demands in *Old Pictures*.

Not the man with the tripod and the sad, snowy steed. He captured what we squandered the summer he came, knowing he'd be gone before we learned what time taught him.

The Slumber Party

December 13, 1989

They came from upper middle-class homes, most of them, the children of doctors, merchants, even the town mayor. They wore their hair straight and their bell-bottoms fringed, sometimes white lipstick. They had their first slumber party when they were 12. Fourteen marriages, 13 children and 25 years later they are still having them.

"We used to talk about who was dating who," began Kay. "Now we talk about who's divorcing who."

No last names please, she asked. A few among the dozen might object to the publicity. So they shall remain simply Kevi, Claudia, Kitty, Jan, Kay, Lou Ann, Kathy, Robyn, Terri, Chris, Marci and Rachel.

Wilmington, Ohio, was home to them; and, because it remains home to most of their parents, it is their annual gathering point for the slumber party.

In the beginning it was pizzas, pop and sloppy Joes. Someone would discreetly tip off the boys so they would sneak over and try to peek in the windows until a parent ran them off.

They conducted seances, revealed deep secrets about themselves during their "true confessions" sessions. The party pooper who first drifted off to sleep was likely to find – the next morning – that her bra had been soaked in water and stuffed in the freezer.

They swapped gossip about who was dating, necking, petting or all of the above. They boldly decided among themselves to sample beer.

"I think we were the only 12 girls," Kay said, laughing, "who could all get drunk on one six-pack."

Using a needle, an ice cube and a bar of soap, they pierced each other's ears.

During their senior year, they decided to have a slumber party along the Ohio River in a camper-trailer belonging to one of their families. Parents insisted on a chaperone, settling upon an older sister of one of the dozen. She showed up with an armload of dirty magazines and a six-pack. That was the night they went skinny-dipping in the Ohio.

They graduated from high school in 1970. Chris, the cheerleader, married the captan of the football team. Each of them began establishing families, careers, separate lives. Somehow, though, they never gave up the slumber party. From as far away as Wisconsin and Texas, they have made the annual trek.

The summons went out again this autumn. Bring your sleeping bag and a bottle of wine. Meet at Kevi's mom's house.

"There's some gray hair," observed Kay, "and some hair that is conspicuously not gray." Now they talk about boys, but it is their sons in college.

The Wilmington mothers who once hosted the slumber parties now babysit the grandchildren during them.

"There is a real bond there," said Kay.

"I know," added Kitty, "that if I picked up the phone in the middle of the night and called Lou Ann and told her that I needed her, she would drive up from Cincinnati."

At the slumber party three years ago, the older sister who had "chaperoned" the skinny-dip surprised her old friends, flying in from Texas, carrying a six-pack and an armload of dirty magazines.

Sure, they still talk about the opposite sex. But, as Kay explained, "It's a more realistic view of the male-female relationship."

Among them, they have come to know their share of tragedy. Miscarriages, failed marriages, a child with birth defects. The parents who once shushed their nightlong parties are aging, and the children they long ago talked about having are now having slumber parties themselves.

At their annual gathering, they do not dwell on the reverses in their lives, disillusionment and doubt, cellulite and wrinkles.

They unroll the sleeping bags and haul out the baby pictures. They recall a time when nothing was as important as knowing who had been spotted necking in a parked car along some lonesome stretch of Oglesby Road. Theirs is a seance to summon the voice of no more cherished an absent friend than youth.

Eulogy for a Cat

April 12, 1989

Old cat, if you had been a human, you would have entered this world the same year Custer made his exit.

I swear, I have no idea what kept you going for so long.

Two years ago, when your feline lifemate was killed by a car, you moped and mourned and nosed around the sun-spangled niches in the house where she had languorously frittered away summer afternoons. But you bounced back, all bad temper and bluster, swatting at the trio of newly adopted kittens, sending the pound puppy yelping for cover when he brazenly stuck a curious nose in your whiskers.

"Charming to the last," I marveled each time your hiss held the other pets at bay, though I swear your breath was worse than your bite.

We thought the cancer would finish you last year. You came home from the vet's office shaven, subdued and sporting more stitches than a baseball.

Your health returned, but never your weight. Surgery did little to ameliorate your mean-spirited eccentricity. You yowled impatiently until your food was set before you. You were the best argument I had for declaring myself a "dog person."

When you, who never had much use for men or dogs, began perching on my lap a few months ago, I was certain that the gesture was attributable to nothing more endearing than a cold draft or a brief lapse in lucidity.

A month ago, old cat, when you stopped eating, ceased complaining, yet were unable to get your fill at the water bowl, I calculated that your time had finally come.

"Poor" was the vet's most charitable prognosis, though he sent you home with antibiotics and issued me a syringe with which to feed you broth. For all of my charm and bedside manner, I got nothing more than a dirty look each time I pried open your jaws to feed you. You rallied, I am convinced, simply to deny me whatever perverse pleasure you imagined I took from those force-feedings. Your recovery was confirmed when you once again began howling at me if I dared to dawdle over my morning coffee before fetching your breakfast.

Debra, my wife, had hoped you would make it until warm weather, recalling 17 summers during which you luxuriated in the grass while your masters sweated out the lawn work.

For one unseasonably warm March weekend she got her wish. But then last weekend you seemed seized by a chill no sun could warm. You huddled in every available lap, rolled yourself into a ball atop laundry still warm from the dryer. And, you stopped eating.

By Sunday afternoon you had difficulty standing, snatched your breath in ragged gasps and seemed totally lost to your surroundings.

When you finally pulled yourself upright Monday morning and proceeded unsteadily to the water dish, I knew you were done. A dim message from somewhere in the fog beyond remembering tried to remind you of why you had come to the water dish, but you sat baffled and uncomprehending. The pup you had once bullied, now grown, sauntered up to the dish and placed his nose up to yours. Getting, for his efforts, not a forepaw swipe but a befuddled stare, he gave you a perfunctory lick behind the ear and walked away.

Debra could not bring herself to make the appointment we both knew could no longer be avoided. She asked only to hold you for a while before you and I left. So I swaddled you in a thick bath towel and found a spot where the sun would warm the couch. One last time, upon hearing – from two rooms away – the voice that had called you for 17 years, you shuddered from your stupor and lifted your proud head to answer.

You went easy, old cat. When the vet placed his stethoscope to your chest I thought about an observation E.B. White once had made about a bewildering confrontation with the death of one of his farm animals.

"I spent several days and nights in mid-September with an ailing pig and I feel driven to account for this stretch of time, more particularly since the pig died at last, and I lived, and things might easily have gone the other way and none left to do the telling."

The telling is done, old cat; though I can't imagine why, as I drink my morning coffee to the news of thousands of creatures dying on Alaska's oil-slick shoals, it is your mean-spirited hide I sense most absent.

Toads Leap Into Crime

June 2, 1989

Just in case you missed the story in Wednesday's *Dispatch*, it is a felony in the United States to lick toads.

Certain types of toads secrete a chemical called bufotinine. Toads release this substance to ward off predators. But somehow, druggies have learned that bufotinine is a mind-altering substance and they have been, well, licking toads to get high.

Imagine this scene:

In the basement of an abandoned Los Angeles house, two young men are seated across from each other at a rickety table upon which a lone candle casts eerie shadows against graffiti-covered walls.

"Are you holding?" the newcomer asked.

The dealer nodded.

"What you got, man?" the junkie pressed. "Crack, smack, coke, grass, 'ludes?"

The dealer shook his head. "Toads," he whispered, removing his sunglasses.

Skeptical, the junkie demanded, "Good toads?"

"Sonoran Desert toads," boasted the dealer. "The best. One lick will blow you away."

"I don't know," said the junkie. "I scored some bad toads from a dude a couple weeks ago. I licked those devils for two hours and didn't get nothin' but this wart on my lip."

"Gotta know your supplier," the dealer said wearily. "Lot of bad toads on the street. People do anything to turn a buck. Guys out there spray painting frogs brown."

"How 'bout a taste?" the junkie ventured.

"Let's see some bread," the dealer replied.

The junkie pulled a handful of wadded bills from his pocket and spread them on the table.

Reaching behind his chair, the dealer lifted a croker sack onto the table and slowly untied the knotted top.

"Been a while?" the dealer taunted. He pulled a fat brown toad from the sack and waved it beneath the junkie's nose.

Hands trembling, the junkie snatched the toad and furtively began licking.

The dealer laughed, "You junkies are all alike. You talk tough till you need a fix, then you'd sell your soul for one good lick. How'd you get started man?"

"I was at a party," the junkie said between slurps. "There were these brownies. I just thought they were regular brownies. One bite and I was fried."

"Easy, man," the dealer said, launching into a familiar refrain, "Don't Bogart that toad, pass him over to me."

The junkie handed over the toad and watched quizzically as the dealer clamped it with what appeared to be an oversized clothes pin.

"Toad clip," the dealer explained. "Keeps 'em from wetting on your hand. First thing the narcs look for is wart tracks. How you feeling, dude?"

"Great, man," came the slurred response. "Except I got the munchies. You got any flies?"

The dealer's laugh was cut short by a clatter of footfalls on the porch upstairs and a shoving at the door.

"Open up!" ordered a voice. "Police!"

"Quick!" screamed the junkie "Flush the toads!"

Too late. The front door splintered and a dozen armed SWAT officers in waterproof vests swarmed down the basement stairs.

The cop flashed his badge, "Sgt. Friday, Los Angeles Police. You're under arrest."

"Aw, man," the dealer complained, "these are just pets."

"Sure, son," Friday responded. "That's what they all say. Frisk 'em boys. Read 'em their rights."

"Look here, Sergeant," called an officer, aiming his flashlight into the croker sack. "These boys were prepared for some serious partying."

Sgt. Friday peered into the bag and shook his head, "Twenty, maybe 30 I'd guess. Street value of $1,000. No misdemeanor boys. You've got more than 15 grams of amphibian here. Aggravated trafficking. Conspiracy to distribute."

The officer at Friday's side shook his head, "When the judge sees this, you guys can kiss the baby."

"Has to taste better than toads," Friday quipped, turning for the stairs. "Let's take 'em downtown."

To Whom It May Concern

October 6, 1989

To whom it may concern:

You got the TV and the VCR. Easy items to fence, I suppose. You took the camera and binoculars, along with two guitars. The only jewelry you left untouched is what Debra was wearing when we walked into the house and discovered the splintered front door. Maxie – no watchdog she, as you doubtless quickly learned – was understandably happy to see us.

Was it worth your risk? I tried to calculate the haul in street math:

Spike steals $4,000 worth of goods. If he fences it for 20 cents on the dollar, and the price of crack is $20 a rock, how soon will he have to hit another house if his habit costs $100 a day?

Let me tell you a little about what you took. You might be able to use it in a sales pitch when you fence it.

The diamond ring was first owned by a proud old woman who fled the Cossacks during a pogrom in Czarist Russia. She came to America with nothing. The ring was purchased with her husband's sweat and handed down three generations.

The guitar, the Guild, is 22 years old. That's an important selling point, in case you don't know. Good wood mellows with age. It has survived two coffeehouses, four bands, and being dropped by a sloshed guest at a wedding reception after her disastrous attempt to sing *Blue Moon of Kentucky*. I'll miss it.

The other guitar was a gift from my brother Joe. He doesn't know yet that's it's gone, and I haven't the heart to call Nashville and tell him.

I think I took the film out of the Canon the day before you got it. I'm still looking around the house for the roll. In case I didn't I don't suppose you'd be considerate enough to drop it in the mail. I can't imagine that photos of my daughter's first homecoming dance would have much street value.

Whoever you are, you have made it possible for me to meet a few people who otherwise would have remained strangers to me. They talk of motion detectors, heat sensors, panic buttons. They quote national crime statistics and speak of "perimeter protection" and "inside traps." It makes burglary sound like the Chicago Bears playbook.

I had to smile when the man from Rollins Protective Services informed me that his company is a steady performer on Wall Street, you being the person in the best position to act on that little market tip. I had to laugh when he told me Rollins also owns Orkin. Both feet in the pest control business.

By the way, I no longer have windows. I have "points of vulnerability." And my points of vulnerability must now be "armed." In short, I now will have to convince a computerized security key pad that it is merely me looking to savor an Indian summer breeze instead of you coming back for what you forgot.

The steel replacement doors have none of the rustic charm of the old wooden Dutch doors. I don't even know if they are any safer. They tell me that if you want to get in, you will.

"Don't you feel violated?" I have been asked by more than one friend since your visit.

Yes, I suppose. Outrage was the first reaction. Then a weary resignation set in. We're all vulnerable. It does no good to rant and rave. I could pen an incensed letter to Congress demanding that something be done about you, but you may be the same person who pulled off one of the four burglaries U.S. Sen. John Glenn has endured.

I've stopped sleeping with the windows open. For a wile, Debra stopped sleeping altogether.

My "personal security analysis questionnaire" inquired, "How long have you owned this house?"

I owned it until sometime around midnight on Sept. 29. Then you became part owner. It became a little investment property for you.

But just in case you get nostalgic (I understand you sometimes do after the 30 days it typically requires for insurance to replace what insurance can), it won't be the same place. It will buzz, beep, wail and summon the police. It won't be the same house you likely remember with a certain warmth and pride of achievement. But then, neither is it for me.

Thanks for the memories, creep.

The Hardens

Five and Dime

November 24, 1989

Lucille Herron placed the bag on the fountain stool to her right and cupped a hand around the bowl of chili before her. She smoothed a $10 bill onto the Formica and sneaked a glance at her watch. She has been a regular at the Woolworth's lunch counter since the days when the bus fare from her Franklinton home to Downtown was 6 cents.

Down the counter, another diner guarding two shopping bags filled with trash scribbled on the back of the paper place mat a conspiratorial note to the waitress about a man seated nearby: "Man...is a full-blooded Indian. Had lived on a reservation in the West."

Frank Woolworth was a 21-year-old clerk in a Watertown, N.Y., dry goods store when an offbeat merchandising idea dawned on him. Why not place all the slow-selling goods on a table at the front of the store and price each item on it a nickel, nothing more? The proprietor, likely skeptical at first, having already reduced Woolworth's $8-a-week salary because of the young man's inept salesmanship, agreed. In that innocent stroke of genius there was born to America a common denominator of retail merchandising, the five and dime.

A thousand Woolworth's dime stores would freckle the national landscape by the time of the founder's death in 1919. Three years later, another would open its doors not far from the dry goods store Simon Lazarus had built on S. High Street.

"Let's say you're going to sell a coffeepot," Arthur Snelling offered. He was seated at a booth near the lunch counter, his hands spread before him as though appraising the fall of cards in a solitaire game only he could see. "The pot is a dime. The stem is a nickel. The basket is a nickel. Each price was marked no more than a dime. Pie was 10 cents. Coffee stayed a dime until 1954 or '55."

Snelling, a Woolworth's assistant manager in his 40th year with the company, is a burly man with a streetwise manner and a head full of company history.

"At one time," he announced brightly, stabbing a finger on the tabletop for emphasis, "Woolworth's sold more hot dogs than anyone else in the world."

It was a decade after the death of Frank Woolworth before the chain was forced to break faith with his edict that nothing be priced higher than a dime. They raised the ceiling to an unthinkable 20 cents.

It is still possible to walk out of the S. High Street Woolworth's carrying 20 cents worth of merchandise. A stone's throw from the trendy, upscale shops and boutiques of the new City Center, a spool of fine thread can be had for a pinched pair of dimes. It is there on the shelf, not far from lampshades and Last Supper prints, toilet seats and goldfish, hula hoops, cowboy hats and parakeets.

In an era of single-minded specialty merchandising, Woolworth's is a retail anachronism – a restaurant that sells hamsters downstairs, a clothing store with hot dogs.

The coin-operated photo booth, a longtime staple of the chain, is temporarily gone from the Downtown store. A new one, capable of shooting a strip of color photos, will arrive in January. The sampling of visages it will capture of Woolworth's shoppers will mirror – perhaps more so than any other retail outlet in the city – an amazing cultural, economic, ethnic and racial plurality. Democracy is a Woolworth's lunch counter at half-past noon.

Diners hunker over hamburgers prepared precisely as they were a half-century ago: grilled three minutes to a side, served with a half-ounce of lettuce and (if requested) a one-eighth-inch slice of Bermuda onion. Cokes arrive in the old-fashioned glasses, shaped like a cropped light bulb and crowned with ice cubes the size of craps dice.

"We're a first-of-the-month store," food manager Jeannie McCrossin said, "a check store. When they get their welfare check or Social Security check, this place is popping."

It is a store that, for a fair measure of its clientele, counts on the COTA buses and watches the skies.

"If it snows or rains, we're dead," McCrossin allowed.

But on the day she spoke, it had been unseasonably warm. A steady procession of shoppers and diners had plied the aisles snooping at everything from Dixie Peach Pomade to postcards of Ohio Stadium.

"White thread, white zippers, chocolate-covered peanuts, shoestrings, razor blades, white handkerchiefs," Arthur Snelling ticked off. At one time he could name 10 items and bet even money that in every F.W. Woolworth's dime store from Bangor to Bakersfield they were the 10 top sellers.

Lucille Herron peeked at her watch and asked the waitress for a to-go container so she could finish her chili later.

Yes, she said, she had seen the City Center.

"Prices are too expensive for me," she sniffed.

She carried her chili and her Woolworth's bag out the front door and past Paul Shaver, a street preacher holding a wood cross in one hand and an upturned tambourine in the other. The cross was aimed at the City Center, as though, as some latter-day disciple of Frank Winfield Woolworth, he was trying to send its shoppers a message about their prodigal ways from his homely perch in front of the five and dime.

Men. Who Needs Them?

January 6, 1991

I was drifting off to sleep the other night when I heard Debra – curled up next to me with Carrie Fisher's *Surrender the Pink* – begin to read aloud:

"The tiny male spider approaches his relatively huge mate and begins to couple. The female devours him in an act of copulatory cannibalism. She chews away the head, leaving the rest of the male's body sexually functional, so his sperm can pass into her body. The male tarantula has a pair of curved appendages on his front legs with which he holds open the female's jaws so that she cannot snap at him during mating."

This is a terribly disturbing bit of information for a male to hear just as he is about to doze off. Yet, I suspect I will hear more as Debra progresses through the book, for each chapter begins with a snippet detailing the mating behavior of a certain species, much of it unflattering to males.

Consider the prelude to Chapter 2:

"With most species of fish, there is little or no contact between the male and the female. The male merely deposits the sperm over the eggs after they've been released by the female. After that brief interlude, the lovers may go their separate ways, never to meet again."

Did you know that foreplay to a male polecat consists of biting his mate on the neck with such ferocity that it causes muscular paralysis?

All of this was disconcerting to me. Suspecting that Carrie Fisher might have singled out those species in which males do not accord themselves proudly, I called the Columbus Zoo hoping for a little ammunition I might use the next time Debra reads me an installment from the book.

What I learned is that males throughout the animal kingdom, whether they slither, crawl, swim or fly, are largely a bunch of inconsiderate slugs indulged by females only because they are a requisite of procreation.

True, there are exceptions. The male seahorse, for instance, is the one who carries the eggs after they have been fertilized. The female places them in his pouch, which, lined with nutrients, sustains them until they hatch.

Consider, by contrast, the male bat. He sometimes awakens frisky in the middle of hibernation and seeks out a female.

Explained Columbus Zoo outreach program coordinator Barbara Ray, "Whether she's awake or not he will go ahead and breed with her."

"They're *guys*!" sniffed a co-worker of mine upon hearing this.

Not only does the bat lack consideration along with any concept of fore-play, he's pretty much a slob when the act is over. Continued Ray, "He physically disengages, but he often falls asleep while he's still hanging on her."

Male opossums signal the urge to mate by making a metallic clicking sound. This is a marsupial version of "Nice band, huh? You come here often?"

"They also slobber on everything," Ray explained with clinical detach-ment. "Then they rub their head and neck in the slobber and they basical-ly look like they just got out of bed."

Thus coiffed do they expect to find an enchanted female. Once they do, they make even bigger fools of themselves. Lost in the moment, they for-get to keep a foot or two on the ground for the sake of balance and often, in the middle of copulation, fall over on their side.

Any woman who has ever been in a singles bar can identify with the mating conduct of snakes. Basically, the male slithers over the female's back sniffing all the while for the pheremones (released by glands in her back) that tell him he may get lucky. Snakes can be very conniving during this process. The male, in certain species, is capable of releasing a phere-mone that smells like that of the female.

Once he releases it, he will sometimes rub it on the backs of other male snakes. Then, while the other males are snuggling up to each other about to make a shocking discovery, he has most of the females to himself.

I peeked ahead in the Carrie Fisher book to learn what I am likely to hear next from Debra and read the following:

"Hippopotamuses can behave very strangely toward each other. A father may bite off the head of his son and a captive adolescent may sud-denly gore his mother to death...That is why the females seek to simplify their domestic lives by staying together, consorting with males only to copulate."

Hey. They're *guys.*

The Fat Man and the Cupcake

May 13, 1991

From the lost manuscripts of Ernest Hemingway, I offer A Clean, Cellulited Place*:*

It was morning, Nick told himself, though it had not always been so. Earlier, it had been night. A man who has lived knows such things and does not question them.

He stood in the shower, which was wet and hot like the warthog he had shot in Kenya, only the warthog did not have a variable speed, pulsating head.

Looking down, Nick was aware that something was missing.

"Toes," he said aloud with a sudden ache, hoping the woman had not heard him. Before the war, he had been able to see his toes. They had been good toes. He liked them. He liked eight of them. The two that had gone "wee, wee, wee" all the way home he could not stand, and he spat at the thought of their cowardice.

He could not see his toes because his stomach was in the way. "Ngai, nagari," his old gun bearer Mokimbo would have said of a man with such paunch "Ngai, nagari," he whispered, translating, "Buddah belly."

He stepped out of the shower unaware that the woman had awakened and was watching him from behind through the open bathroom door.

"Hills like white elephants," she laughingly pointed, throwing back her head in a way she did when he had taken her to the little cafe overlooking the Seine and, using his rusty Berlitz French, had mistakenly ordered "a pair of road-killed armadillos and two adult diapers for me and my little emu." The waiter had laughed and it had gone badly.

Now the woman was laughing again. There would be no Fruit Loops for breakfast. The woman would make him drink the Slim-Fast and eat the little sandwiches of alfalfa sprouts that a certain kind of man must eat when he can no longer see his toes.

"You will need me to tie your shoes again," she dryly observed.

"It has not always been so," he said.

"You have forgotten, perhaps, the fat farm in Arkansas?" she reminded him.

He winced at the thought. At the fat farm in Arkansas he could not eat as he had always eaten. At night, the nurses would come and search his belongings. It had cost him three dozen cakes on whose boxes was a picture of a girl who was little and whose name was Debbie. At the fat farm he could not get the little plastic containers of nachos as he had in the old days when he went to see the Indians of Cleveland or the Tigers of Detroit. The nachos had been good then. They were covered with something the vendors called "cheese" even though it had never seen a cow.

"What will you have?" the woman asked him at the breakfast table.

If she were gone he would be pouring Yoo-Hoo chocolate drink over Count Chocula.

"Toast, straight up" he answered hoarsely. "Will it always be this way?"

She sniffed, "It must, until you no longer need a mirror to see if your socks match."

"You are a cruel one," he scowled.

"And you are big enough to have your own ZIP code," she shot back.

She placed the toast before him and he ate it slowly and with none of the gusto with which he had seen lions devouring Baptist missionaries. He swallowed hard. At this point in his diet Baptist missionaries were starting to look good.

When the woman had left for work, he removed his game pouch from the closet and sneaked to the convenience store.

"You again, *Ingles*?" smiled the clerk whose name had too many consonants, but who could sing Wagnerian arias in farsi. "How many?" he asked placing his hands on the Twinkies.

"*Dos*," Nick said, looking over his shoulder. "And be quick about it."

The clerk sneered.

"Ambrosia," Nick said when he had ripped through the wrapper and stuffed the cake into his mouth.

"Will you have some to go?" the clerk inquired.

"Yes," he answered. "and I will have the Hostess Sno Balls, too; the ones that are white and resemble Kilimanjaro except that Kilimanjaro does not have coconut and a cream filling."

No Home In This World Anymore

November 5, 1990

They sat, rawboned and sallow, aged less by the years than the mileage. Five o'clock stubbles wreathed frowns on faces weathered as barnwood. Rheumy eyes, too long accustomed to refracting life through a muscatel haze, fixed upon a young troubadour who echoed their anthem off the marble floor of the homeless shelter.

"I ain't got no home in this world anymore," he sang.

Woody Guthrie penned it more than a half-century ago for the hardscrabble nomads of another generation. It was a timely refrain for the Depression years they spent trainbound for something less than glory. We are still trying to sort out what the staying power of the lyrics ought to tell us about our time and ourselves. It was an apt lament Thursday night at the Volunteers of America shelter where the homeless have assembled every year for 13 autumns to conduct a requiem Mass for fallen sparrows.

One was asphyxiated in March in a dumpster off Town Street where he had made his berth. Some say he was smoking. Some think he had lit a fire to stay warm.

One bled to death in a Downtown railroad tunnel.

One died of a heart attack. A wizened carny, he had sought refuge in the shelter when he grew too old for the circuit.

One breathed his last in an alley near the shelter.

"These men died alone and unmourned," began shelter director Graham LeStourgeon. "Let us remember the names of men who don't have a home in this world anymore."

James Bryson, William Farris, Fred Sullivan, Ernest Carpenter.

LeStourgeon talked a little about each, a little being all most people knew about the quartet. A man can be stingy with his life's story when it is one he would just as soon forget.

Continuing, LeStourgeon recited the names of 116 more homeless dead who had been lost since the inception of the annual memorial service.

Many of them had warmed the same drab folding chairs this year's mourners occupied. Here and there, next to their alphabetized names on the nine-page necrology, a brief comment about their lives and how they ended had been recorded for many:

"A suicide uptown at the age of 20," noted a comment on one. Another was remembered as "a pleasant, mild-mannered fellow who went fishing on the bank of the Scioto River, got drunk and rolled into the water and drowned."

"Died the day after Easter when he was run over by a train," recalled one more.

Most of the absolute superlatives that might have been borrowed for a eulogy for many of the men were hardly flattering. For in their hardest hours none had fallen further, gotten drunker or been dogged by more demons. But LeStourgeon had dug until he found something charitable to say.

"He came from a fine South Side family," he recalled of one, "and he knew his Lutheran catechism."

LeStourgeon's determination not to judge lives he had not lived called to mind the funeral prayer for a dead Okie in Steinbeck's *The Grapes of Wrath*:

"This here ol' man jus' lived a life an jus' died out of it. I don't know whether he was good or bad, an' it don't matter much. Heard a fella say a poem once, an' he says, 'All that lives is holy.'"

The homeless listened as LeStourgeon read the 90th Psalm. Among their faces most likely were a few that will be remembered at next year's service.

It is hard to imagine them begging for spare change without recalling that the mythological Charon refused to ferry the dead across the River Styx until the tribute of a coin had been placed beneath their lifeless tongues.

"I ain't got a home in this world anymore," sang young Matt Ballin to a room of sympathetic ears.

Home.

If, as the Bible tells us, "His eye is on the sparrow," four of their kind have finally found one.

Field of Dreams

June 28, 1993

DYERSVILLE, Iowa – The Rev. Gabriel Anderson, a lanky young priest with an easy manner and a beatific smile, spread his arms – as if embracing the foul lines of the Dyersville area's most famous baseball diamond – and, to salute the pioneers who built his church in 1888, invoked a familiar quotation.

"A very small number of parishioners built a very large church," he began, "because they believed that if they built it, people would come. They were only 225 families, but they believed that, if they built a beautiful and magnificent church, God would bless their families and their farms."

"It's a spiritual version of *Field of Dreams*," said the Rev. Thomas Francis, a visiting priest from Georgia who had dropped by to see the film site.

He seemed pleased to have plucked an analogy from the Iowa skies that promised the fictional Ray Kinsella, as he strolled through the high corn: "If you build it, they will come."

Whether their business is salvation, tourism or souvenir saltshakers, more than a few people in Dyersville want a piece of the dream.

The Dyersville Area Chamber of Commerce has produced a slick promotional package touting everything from a toy factory to a woodcarving museum (not to mention Anderson's Basilica of St. Francis Xavier), borrowing another *Field of Dreams* line: "Is this heaven?"

Not likely. A heaven with property lines is hard to imagine. And, on Dyersville's famous field, the property line is everything.

Don Lansing owns the infield, right field and part of center on what was the movie set. His neighbors, Al and Rita Ameskamp, own left field and the other half of center.

Both Ameskamps and Lansing have concession stands. Both sell T-shirts and souvenirs.

Longtime, Dyersville neighbors, they seem to have become competitors since the filming of *Dreams* in 1988. They seem to show one another the strained civility and transparent politeness displayed by border guards of hostile, neighboring countries.

Lansing erected his souvenir stand first. The Ameskamps opened theirs a year ago.

"We get along fine," Al Ameskamp said from inside his cabooselike concession stand, "but we each do our own thing."

A sign reminds visitors to the Ameskamp's portion of the field: "We are not associated with the other souvenir stand."

Pointing to a spot in the sky above center field, Ameskamp explained, "Where the power line goes through here, that is the dividing line of the property."

Each spring, Ameskamp climbs onto his tractor and plants corn in his share of the outfield. Lansing does the same.

Lansing offers T-shirts emblazoned "Is this heaven? No, it's Iowa."

The Ameskamps' T-shirts do not bear that legend, but, unlike Lansing, they hawk peanuts and Cracker Jacks.

Lansing has "Shoeless Joe" playing cards and *Field of Dreams* shot glasses. The Ameskamps have the official *Field of Dreams* baseball bat and wristwatch.

Into the midst of these dueling concession stands, one hot June day, wandered the Casey family of La Crescent, Minn. – father Ken, mother Delaine, 11-year-old son Tim and 7-year-old daughter Nicole.

Oblivious to the competition surrounding them, they strolled out to the diamond and knocked the ball around for an hour or so.

What drew them to Dyersville is the idea that occasionally has visitors standing reverently in the Ameskamps' high corn at 1 a.m.

It is an idyllic notion about baseball and a romanticization of the mystical and magical.

It doesn't square with the greedy cat fight that major-league baseball has become or the "friendly" competition at the movie site.

But the Caseys understand that baseball was never intended to be about labor strikes, arbitration, spiritual salvation or $5 salt-and-pepper shakers.

And maybe that's all that matters.

Death of a Bluesman

July 2, 1993

LELAND, Miss. – James "Son" Thomas didn't die the sort of death that would inspire a funky, 12-bar eulogy from his blues-playing contemporaries.

The death certificate doesn't say anything about women, whiskey or "working for the man" – but anyone who knew Thomas was aware that, while none of those changed his age, they certainly put some miles on the odometer.

Tethered to the tubes and intravenous lines that sustained what some might call life after his massive stroke of a month ago, the 66-year-old Thomas blessedly succumbed on Saturday.

For a man who once dodged every bullet but one fired by a gun-toting, spurned woman who interrupted a gig with some percussion of her own (the shot in the side left him "stoved up" for a while, he said), he exited quietly at a place called the Autumn Leaves Convalescent Center.

He lived long enough to be "discovered" twice by well-intentioned white patrons of Delta blues and primitive art (having turned out sculptures fashioned of gumbo clay since boyhood). He was even received at the White House by former first lady Nancy Reagan, who praised his craftsmanship at sculpting. No doubt he was dissuaded from showing up with one of his clay "death heads" with human teeth.

Despite the art shows and the proceeds from record sales, when Thomas suffered the stroke that eventually claimed him, he was still living in a shotgun house on Hutson Street in a section of Leland that the locals call "Black Dog."

He was schooling his son, Dwayne, the 11th of his 13 children, in sculpting.

The younger Thomas' sculptures, like those of his father, trade excessively on death as an artistic motif: men in caskets, hollow-eyed skulls.

"He talked about death a lot," Dwayne acknowledged. "First piece he taught me was a small casket. I sold it for $10."

The elder Thomas may have talked a lot about death because he made part of his living in his salad days as a $15-a-week gravedigger.

Dwayne suggested that, because the paltry salary was enhanced when business was brisk, "Son" earned a reputation for dropping in on folks to inquire about the condition of the aged and infirm.

Son learned to play guitar on a Gene Autry flattop. Many of the blues numbers he sang before he began writing lyrics, he learned from 78-rpm records spun on an aging, windup gramophone. That record player frightened his grandfather who believed that its sound horn was a crude transmitter used by white folks to eavesdrop on the household conversations of their sharecroppers.

Son scorned that foolish notion as much as he mocked the dark fable that a Rt.61 blues man could trade his soul to the devil for fame – if he hammered out the details of the arrangement at midnight beneath a certain tree at a crossroads along the old route hugging the Mississippi River.

"I never did pay any attention to talk like that," he once said.

The eulogy delivered over the remains of Son Thomas at Leland's Jerusalem Temple Church of God in Christ will, no doubt, skirt incidents that suit juke-joint lyrics.

Dwayne Thomas smilingly concurred that his father did not spend an excessive amount of time warming church pews anywhere in the Delta.

"Beefsteak when I'm hungry," Son used to sing, "and whiskey when I'm dry / Goodlooking women whilst I'm living, and heaven when I die."

If you have something important to say about life, sing it in the first verse. You never can tell when a woman with a gun might interrupt the second.

Dopey Dog

December 29, 1992

My dog is not speaking to me. She'll get over it, I'm sure, but it's all my fault.

Regular readers may recall that my dog, Maxie, is epileptic. I wrote a column about her several weeks ago, when her seizures began to worsen and the medication to control them wasn't doing the job. Several readers wrote or called with suggestions for controlling the epilepsy, and I am grateful for their concern and counsel.

The good news is that Maxie hasn't had a seizure lately. That is no small miracle, given an act of carelessness on my part.

Let me explain.

Earlier this month, while I was in Russia, my veterinarian took a look at Maxie to see what could be done to reduce the seizures. He did a liver study to find out whether the dog's phenobarbital dosage could be increased without undue risk, and he determined that it could.

"Maxie's on a different kind of pill," my wife, Debra, told me when I returned from Moscow. "It is on the kitchen counter."

In my absence, Debra had been medicating the dog, but she was only too happy to relinquish the task.

I was still suffering jet lag the first morning I opened the pill bottle and summoned the dog. A bit startled by the size of the pill, I nonetheless managed to get it down Maxie.

On the third day, Maxie began acting a little spacey. Her behavior reminded me of a dog I had written about several years ago that had eaten a marijuana-laced brownie.

Maxie is normally a fairly rambunctious dog. When she spots a squirrel in the back yard from her perch on the couch, her hackles rise, and her barking doesn't cease until the interloper is gone.

With the new medication, though, her attitude seemed to change. If dogs could talk, she would have said, "Oh, wow, a squirrel. I can groove on that."

For years, Maxie has slept at the foot of my bed, but that ended with the new medication. She would stare at the bed as if she dimly remembered that she once knew how to get up there. Yet she was incapable of the jump.

A friend who dropped by noticed that, when Maxie tried to scratch her ear with her hind leg, she missed.

I decided to take a closer look at the label on the bottle of medicine prescribed by the vet. I was not surprised to see that it includes a warning about drowsiness.

Then I thought: Wait a minute. Why would a vet think it prudent to warn a four-legged patient about not trying to operate heavy machinery while taking a medication?

Then I noticed that the pills I had been giving Maxie were not her new anti-convulsant; they were, rather, a muscle relaxant prescribed for Debra's chronic shoulder pain.

I phoned the vet.

He told me that, in addition to baby-sitting a dog who would act like a junkie for a while, I ought to be concerned about stomach upset (one of the side effects of the muscle relaxant).

"How should I treat that?" I inquired.

"Got any Maalox?" he said.

Dogs, I have discovered the past several days, do not obligingly drink Maalox. We wrestled a bit over the matter, and I finally was forced to squirt it onto the back of her tongue with a small syringe.

At this writing, she is recovering nicely. She is able to climb onto the bed again, bark at squirrels and scratch where it itches.

And, despite the mix-up in medications, she hasn't had a seizure for a while.

Come to think of it, neither has Debra. I wonder whose medicine *she* was taking.

Cross Dressing Actuaries Who Can't Say "No."

March 15, 1992

I see by the TV listing that this week Oprah has "unusual sexual and behavioral habits." Sally is hosting "parents who disapprove of their children getting a tattoo." Geraldo will talk about "hiring a P.I. to investigate a spouse or lover's infidelities."

Pretty tame subjects for that trio. I'm more accustomed to the kinds of guests who make ax murderers watching television on death row leap up and shout, "Where do they *get* these people?"

How do they come up with these topics?

I have a theory. Let's just call it the Chinese menu theory of talk-show programming. I am willing to wager that if you were able to sneak into the office of the producer of *Sally Jessy Raphael* you would find a dartboard that, instead of a standard bull's-eye, features three columns of words.

When it comes time to plan topics for an upcoming month, the producer, feet propped up on the desk, simply pulls out his darts and lofts, one toward Column A.

Here are the listings for Column A:
1. Dysfunctional
2. Cross-dressing
3. Incontinent
4. Workaholic
5. Bisexual
6. Born-again
7. Transsexual
8. Hermaphrodite
9. Logorrheic
10. Republican
11. Narcoleptic
12. Claustrophobic
13. Shoplifting
14. Networking
15. Psychic

At this point, the producer makes a note of the number in Column A closest to where his dart landed and then throws another for Column B:
1. Bikers
2. Actuaries
3. Plumbers
4. Pimps
5. Agnostics
6. Klansmen
7. Nuns
8. Vegetarians
9. Mistresses
10. Necrophiles
11. Presbyterians
12. Nannies
13. Podiatrists
14. Krishnas
15. Gigolos

Ah, now we're on a roll. The producer has a number from Column A and another from Column B. To this combination he adds the word "who" and moves on to Column C:
1. Abuse laxatives
2. Enjoy phone sex
3. Collect butterflies
4. Slam-dance
5. Lick toads
6. Can't say "no"
7. Flog hamsters
8. Sing opera
9. Drool uncontrollably
10. Have spotted Elvis
11. Steal hubcaps

12. Chose divorce
13. Slept with Warren Beatty
14. Suffer from loose dentures
15. Have been here before

Voila! As easy as ABC, you have "narcoleptic Klansmen who abuse laxatives" or "hermaphrodite plumbers who flog hamsters." How about "born-again vegetarians who have spotted Elvis" or "dysfunctional Republicans who slept with Warren Beatty" or "bisexual podiatrists who drool uncontrollably"?

Unfortunately, even with the vast number of combinations possible, a producer will eventually exhaust them all. What then? He goes to his recycle list. The recycle list is very short. It includes "children of," "adult children of," "parents of" and "spouses of."

Thus does the producer append the theme of one of his old shows and end up with "adult children of narcoleptic Klansmen who abuse laxatives" or "spouses of dysfunctional Republicans who slept with Warren Beatty."

Of course, that might require a bit of clarification on Oprah's part. Otherwise, it is unclear whether it is the adult child or the narcoleptic Klansman who is abusing the laxatives. Same problem comes up in clarifying just who it is who slept with Warren Beatty.

I can't wait to see "psychic nuns who steal hubcaps."

"The Black Dog"

March 18, 1991

Her mother named her Martha, but her husband, Joe, always called her Mart, as in "You'll have to excuse Mart; she ain't quite up to snuff lately," or "Don't mind Mart. It's her nerves."

She was my mother-in-law for 17 years, and, for many of them, she battled what Winston Churchill once called "the black dog" – depression.

"She's good now," her daughter, Suzanne, told me when I first came to Pittsburgh so that Mart could meet her prospective son-in-law.

We got along famously. She loved good music, good food and good times. I found it difficult to believe the stories I had heard about her depression. Sadly, they were all true enough.

She first battled it almost 50 years ago and fought it episodically ever after that. Perplexed doctors tried everything that came down the pike: Librium, Valium, Lithium, Tofranil, Elavil. I don't know how many times she had shock treatments. She was variously diagnosed as suffering from depression, manic-depression, agitated depression.

In the beginning, the "highs" outlasted the "lows" enough to invite the hope that maybe, just maybe, it was a problem she could put behind her.

But the floor of the valley grew longer each time, the plateaus lower and shorter.

As much as her grace, charm and zest for life were contagious during her good days, so her agitation was during the bad.

"What is she like?" Suzanne's current husband, John, asked me as he prepared to meet her during one of her bad times.

"She's no box of chocolates," I confided. It was a calloused, unfeeling appraisal, but it was true.

All of those years of emotional torture took a toll. Studying a photo taken of her at her 50th anniversary brunch and recalling a time when she was healthy, vital and at peace with her demons, I whispered, "My God. How few clues the raisin gives us about the lushness of the grape."

But then a strange thing happened. She was stricken with terminal cancer. And, at a time when one would have thought she would most need that prescription fruit salad of mood elevators and tranquilizers, she needed it not one bit.

The bark of antagonism was gone, along with the veil of depression that had clouded many of her years.

With stunning clarity she could see the reality of the moment. She began making her peace, confiding to a nurse about her husband and her daughters, "I'm not ready just quite yet. When I am, I'll tell them."

She said it not with anger but with a serene determination.

She even showed glimpses of that fine, self-deprecating sense of humor so rarely seen in the last years.

"Mom, you look real good," Suzanne told her toward the end.

"Where the hell are you looking?" Mart teasingly answered.

Seeing her mother's agony during the last days, Suzanne told her, "Mom, I know how much you must love me if you can suffer so much pain and still want to be with me.

"It's all right, Mom," her daughter Bonnie consoled her. "You can let go now."

At her bedside for the last time, her husband, Joe, kissed his fingertips and touched them to her cheek, "I really do love you," he murmured.

"I know you do," she told him. "I know you do."

Suddenly all of the days of emotional torture seemed not only to be distant history but also a history that belonged to anyone other than Mart as in "You'll have to excuse Mart. It's her nerves, you know."

Some might think it a cruel trick for her to regain her emotional health at the moment when her physical health numbered the days she could savor it."

"I must go," she said. "I must go home."

We sighed and wrung our hands and lamented the fact that the curtain was coming down.

It was strange. Because, at the very end, she acted for all the world as though it was just going up.

On Cold Winter Nights

February 22, 1993

As a child I spent many an uneasy winter night studying the shadowed outline of icicles hanging from eaves, illuminated against a window blind by a nearby street light.

I thought those icicles the talons of a hideous beast – half dragon, half bird – waiting for me to drift off to sleep before plunging a claw through the frost-edged pane and snatching me from beneath my covers.

If but momentarily I shifted my gaze from the talons, then looked back, I could swear that they had moved – subtly, barely perceptibly but certainly.

Forty years removed from my irrational fear, I now spend the waning days of February fearing not that I will be snatched from the snug safety inside but that I will be held hostage forever within it.

We are prisoners at this time of year, "clients" of some meteorological correctional system, whose incarceration brings on symptoms we jokingly call those of "cabin fever" because "stir-crazy" hits too close to home.

At such times, clocks tick too loudly, and botched fingerings at the piano can be heard rooms away. The timbers and beams of the house murmur their insomnia as they settle in for the night. And always, at moonrise, from somewhere deep in the thick of the woods, comes a feral baying that bristles the neck hairs.

Somewhere, lost among the boxes of books stacked in my garage, is an oversize volume titled *Wisconsin Death Trip*. It is chock-full of weathered photographs of the rugged but ragged countenances of those who tamed this land. Several passages chronicle the madness and mayhem that befell early settlers of the Midwestern frontier when the cold, the isolation and the encroaching walls of sod houses became too much for them.

Coatless, shoeless, they ran frothing into the unrelenting embrace of winter storms, their bodies discovered only after the first thaw.

Fit, sane and hearty at harvest time, what drove them insane before winter yielded to spring?

Unforgiving, the cold and gray hem us into a corner of our psyche where nothing feels comfortable. Like deer caught straddling the center line by the headlights of a fast-approaching car, we are momentarily stunned, incapable of flight.

I stare at things when winter has kept me cooped up too long, lose the thread of simple conversations until perplexed glances suggest that I have been asked a question I didn't hear.

This unfocused detachment rarely lasts long. In its absence, conversely, is a heightened sensory awareness attuned less to what is harmonious than to what is discordant or slightly out of place.

Time seems out of order. Only two weeks ago, Columbus construction workers were braving a February afternoon shirtless. Now the wind chill dips to negative double digits.

As well as I know the diagnosis, I know the cure: spring.

Cabin fever turns petty grievances into full-blown arguments because windows cannot be thrown open to a cross breeze that would carry off the stagnant rancor within.

Even the cats grow restless, snapping and batting at one another when feeding time is even slightly delayed, hogging the one spot on the couch where infrequent shafts of sunlight fall. It has been months since they heard a bird or trapped a helpless moth inside a lampshade. They're going a bit bats.

Double-paned windows shut out the sounds that lull me to sleep: train whistles and owls, rain on the roof. They keep everything out but the dogs in the distance.

The afternoon yawns. Dinnertime approaches. A fading sun has shrunk the icicles hanging from the gutter out the back window. But they are not gone.

If one studies them long enough, with dusk approaching, one can see a slight, barely noticeable movement, as if they were flexing in preparation for the coming night.

So Bad They're Good

March 22, 1993

Before we announce this year's winners of the fifth annual Worst Country Music Song Titles of All Time Until the Next Time, let us pause for a word from the accounting firm of Kermit, Kermit, Bert, Bert, Ernst & Ernst & Miss Piggy:

The nominees for this year's WCMSTOATUTNT awards were chosen by a distinguished panel of judges selected from addressees whose Publishers Clearing House notices were returned marked "Insufficient Address" and dumped at a landfill. Final winners were chosen from nominated titles using a complex and painstaking process, during which 14 residents of Nashville's 16th Avenue Lighthouse Mission were asked to spit watermelon seeds at computer printouts.

Until this morning, the winners were known to only the accountants and a handful of senior citizens taking a psychic-awareness course at the Days Inn next door.

The winners:

The Worst You Ever Gave Me Was the Best I Ever Had
Does Steppin' Out Mean Daddy Took a Walk?
I'm Ashamed To Be Here (But Not Ashamed Enough To Leave)

Your Alibi Called Today
It Took a Lot of Drinkin' (To Get That Woman Over Me)
Whoever Turned You On Forgot To Turn You Off
I've Got You on My Conscience But at Least You're Off My Back
Velcro Arms, Teflon Heart
If the Jukebox Took Teardrops (I'd Cry All Night Long)
I'm the One She Missed Him With Today
Ten Years, Three Kids and Two Loves Too Late
Touch Me With More Than Your Hands
Walk Out Backwards Slowly So I'll Think You're Walkin' In
I Keep Forgettin' That I Forgot About You
I Don't Know Whether To Kill Myself (Or Go Bowling)
I'll Marry You Tomorrow, But Let's Honeymoon Tonight
It Ain't Love But It Ain't Bad
Walkin', Talkin', Cryin', Barely Beatin' Broken Heart
Is It Cold in Here (Or Is It Just You)?
Normally, Norma Loves Me
Get Your Biscuits in the Oven and Your Buns in the Bed
You Won't Be Back But George and Jack Will Help Me Make It Through the Night
How Can a Whiskey 6 Years Old Whip a Man That's 32?
How Come Your Dog Don't Bite Nobody but Me?
If You Don't Believe I Love You, Just Ask My Wife
I've Been Roped and Throwed by Jesus in the Holy Ghost Corral
Get Your Tongue out of My Mouth Because I'm Kissing You Goodbye
Come Back to Us, Barbara Lewis Hare Krishna Beauregard
I Love the Way He Left You
Defrost Your Heart
Bad Girls Don't Have Suntans
You Make My Heart Want a Dip of Snuff
The Pint of No Return
I Got In at 2 With a 10 and Woke Up at 10 With a 2
Her Body Couldn't Keep You Off My Mind
Do You Love as Good as You Look?
I've Been Flushed from the Bathroom of Your Heart
You're Going to Ruin My Bad Reputation
If I Ain't Got It (You Don't Need It)
Make Me Late for Work Today
I'm All He's Got (But He's Got All of Me)
Katy Did and Dinah Might
She Can't Get My Love off the Bed
Hell Stays Open All Night
All I Want From You (Is Away)
I Wish I Could Hurt That Way Again
If Fingerprints Showed Up on Skin (Wonder Whose I'd Find on You)

If the Phone Doesn't Ring, It's Me
Somebody Must Have Loved You Right Last Night
If Whiskey Were a Woman I'd Be Married for Sure
We Used To Kiss on the Lips But Now It's All Over

What Women Want To Hear

July 12, 1993

In the afternoon, Nick would go to the pool where he had gone with the woman in the old days.

It was a good pool and blue, though the water was no good for drinking. The one-eyed Basque, the pool boy, had once seen Nick cupping his hands to taste it and laughed, "Ha! Ingles. Los ninos, they go pssss."

The woman would have smiled at that. She was a good woman who smoked crooked cigarillos and drank her scotch neat. Her name was Blaze or Blair and she was androgynous. He liked that in a woman. But she had left like all the others.

"Just what is it that you women want today?" he had asked too loudly as they sat beneath the umbrella of the sidewalk cafe along Rue Ennui.

She had spat and called for her check, and suddenly he had felt very old.

Now, at the pool, he thought about the question again. He could ask the lifeguard who was bronze and handsome. But he had probably turned his brain to rubber cement with steroids.

Not far from the towel he had spread on the grass near the pool, two women sat talking quietly. He took them to be American, for when he had arrived they nodded politely, then looked at one another with bored smiles and together said, "Not!" He couldn't understand this, but he knew it was not good.

Now they had risen and gone to the pool. He smiled slyly to himself. He would find out what today's woman really wants, he thought, reaching across the grass for the pair of American magazines they had left on the beach towel.

"*Good Housekeeping*," he murmured quietly to himself.

Quickly, he removed the stub of a pencil from his rucksack, along with an old envelope from the Hotel Bienville.

He scribbled quickly each sentence: "Smooth lashes with absolutely no clumping," "protects against freezer burn" and "without any greasy mess or hassle."

Tossing aside the *Good Housekeeping*, he grabbed hungrily for the *Redbook*. It was a month old. He sighed heavily. Perhaps women had not changed what they want since June.

With the blunt stub he copied, "Extra deodorant protection that won't fade away" and "No mixing, no messy specimen cups" and "for the fit, comfort and incomparable freedom of Lycra."

He returned the magazines to the towel where he had found them and, rising, put on his sunglasses and sucked in his stomach.

"Now," he told himself, "you must go to the concession stand and find a woman and see if these things are so."

He was secretly pleased that the line in front of him was long. He queued up behind a handsome woman with cascading auburn hair. He wondered whether her suit was of true, 100 percent Lycra.

Impatient, she glanced from side to side. When she removed her sunglasses, he seized the opportunity.

"Smooth lashes with absolutely no clumping," he winked, shaking a Camel from the pack and cupping his hand against the wind to light it. "You are American, no?"

She laughed, looking away.

He did not know whether that was a good sign.

The line was moving quickly, and he tried to think of something else.

"Some things a woman cannot hide," he said, pretending to be studying the trees. "You want safe, gentle, dependable action that works even while you sleep. Is this not so?"

Again she turned away, annoyed.

"We can go away," he invited. "There will be no more tangles or split ends, no messy specimen cups."

"Creep!" she hissed.

The other women in the line turned quickly.

Nervously, he fingered the gold chain at his throat and pretended to adjust the waistband of his Speedo.

He forced a so-what smile. In the old days he would have laughed – "C'est La vie" or "Que sera, sera" – but these were not the old days.

What could he say? It would have to be something all-knowing and wise, for they were all staring at him.

"Stains find kids," he said, laughing, perhaps a bit too loudly. "Oxydol finds stains."

Aunt Gracie's Advice

May 26, 1993

My Dear Nephew Mike,

I hear by way of your Momma that you have a pair of young'uns about to graduate from high school next week.

Seems not long ago that you were down here at Methane High School in a cap and gown, singing the alma mater and fight song one last time (you've probably forgotten the words to Roll O Mighty Hustlin' Slugs).

Anyway, I suppose I could send your kids a couple of books of McDonald's gift certificates, but -- as they step out into this cruel, hard world -- that wouldn't get them much beyond tomorrow's lunch.

So I hope you'll pass along a little of their Aunt Gracie's advice for getting along in life.

First, try to keep them out of politics. You've read a bit of Mark Twain, so you know that -- excepting Congress -- America doesn't have what he called "a distinctly criminal class."

But, just in case they decide that Capitol Hill can't live without them, remind them that nothing is more annoying to a congressman who's gotten too big for his britches than us folks back in the home district who knew he was getting in over his head when he quit his job as a clerk for the county extension agent.

It's been said before, but you can tell your two to remember the little folks -- because they'll help them on their way up and meet them on their way down.

College is going to give them a whole bunch of chances to do some stupid things with people who smash beer cans on their foreheads, paint their faces scarlet and gray and go waist-up naked at November football games. Just tell them not to do anything they wouldn't want photographed and shown to their children in 10 years.

If they decide they're going to major in fine arts, creative writing, theater or something else along the artsy-fartsy lines, make sure they know how to bag groceries. You don't need them moving back home when they're 30 because they -- what's the expression? -- don't want to "prostitute their talent."

While they're in college, they'll probably have a lot of people calling up or dropping by who want to talk to them about "securing their financial future."

Take it from Aunt Gracie: It doesn't pay to have any more life insurance than it takes to pay the undertaker. Too much life insurance can put all kinds of scheming thoughts into the head of a spouse who sits watching *Jeopardy*! while her significant other is at a Motel 6, talking about how terrible it is to be misunderstood at home.

Tell them to take time for themselves. I know people who bust their butts making sure everybody is happy except themselves. What they miss doesn't hit them until their chances to let it all hang out have shrunk to yelling "bingo!" at the senior center.

When it gets to be time for them to think about such things, you might have them consider a living will. It never struck me as important until one morning when I watched *Today*.

If I make it to 99, then start falling apart, I don't want a well-meaning relative to keep me plugged in if all I've got to live for is the chance to get a 100th birthday hello from Willard Scott.

Finally, remind the kids of what Roger Miller -- God rest that boy -- said about living and dying.

He said it don't matter how big or important we get in life; the size of our funeral is going to depend more or less on the weather.

I don't know about you, but I'm hoping for a rainy day when my time comes. That way I'll have an excuse if attendance is sparse.

My best to your Momma.

Love,

Aunt Gracie

A Small Piece of History

May 23, 1993

SHARPSBURG, Md. – The wide brick farmhouse beside the road leading to town rests partially hidden among the trees, away from passing motorists.

Those who ascribe human qualities to brick and mortar might liken it to an uncle who dawdles on the fringe of a family reunion so others won't glimpse too closely a suit that is no longer fashionable.

Accordingly, it was the work of those more concerned with substance than progress that had the most to do with saving the old house.

More than 130 years ago, on the land upon which the house looks out, there occurred an event of no small consequence to the Civil War.

It was there, in the fall of 1862, that an impatient Abraham Lincoln sat down with Gen. George McClellan, after the bloodiest single-day battle in the war, and listened for one good reason not to fire the commander of the Union Army.

McClellan had defeated Gen. Robert E. Lee's troops days earlier in the battle of Antietam, but the cost had been staggering. The Union had counted more than 2,000 dead, with 10,000 others wounded or missing. Rebels had been sent fleeing, but the timid McClellan – despite Lincoln's urging – had not followed to finish them off.

When word reached Lincoln that McClellan had not moved in for the kill because his horses were fatigued and sore-tongued well after the time they needed to rest, Abe wired his military chief, "Will you pardon me for asking what the horses of your army have done since the battle of Antietam that fatigues anything?"

The oft-reprinted photograph of Lincoln and McClellan's meeting – like so many official photographs of presidents – doesn't reveal the heavy agenda on the mind of the chief executive. One must look hard at Lincoln's expression to catch the restrained contempt he harbored for McClellan's timidity. To the naive beholder, Lincoln looks strangely calm.

McClellan didn't know that the president had already decided to fire him. Otherwise, he might not have written his wife boasting that Lincoln "was very affable and I really think he does feel very kindly towards me personally."

Lincoln might have been thinking about all the Union dead whose bodies – in final, frozen repose – had been captured by the camera of Matthew Brady. Those macabre pictures were being sold as Civil War souvenirs on the streets of New York City – not much of an enlistment incentive.

McClellan had to go.

One final time, the general reviewed the troops camped on the land that the farmhouse overlooks, then went home to plot his bid to unseat Lincoln.

In time, the land was returned to more pastoral business – that is, until someone thought it might make a good site for a mini-mall, perhaps, or a muffler shop.

Sharpsburg old-timers, along with a few newcomers of similar inclinations, decided to fight it.

Granted, it wasn't as if someone wanted to level the Lincoln Memorial for a yogurt stand, but sometimes a small claim to history is enough ammunition against the encroachment of plastic-and-chrome progress.

The Sharpsburg preservationists won.

That's good -- because they weren't a bunch of frothing NIMBYs. They were just people who care a little more about history than the ready convenience of taco stands.

If the descendants of George McClellan are unsettled that a chance to camouflage the site of their ancestor's professional Waterloo has been lost -- too bad.

Some of us want to show the kids the spot where Lincoln bit the bullet and McClellan bit the dust.

Sometimes, just keeping the quiet grass where it happened is more important than building a shop to sell Honest Abe souvenir ashtrays.

When I Am Old

May 12, 1993

As I study the beeping cursor, my thoughts are on a Jane Casey poem titled *When I Am an Old Man I'll Wear Plaid.*

Shared with me by Ellie Barr, one of the dear hearts and gentle people down in Kingston, Ohio, the poem might more aptly be titled When I Am an Old Man I'll Get Even -- for its chief message is that life (if we're lucky) eventually confers upon us a shot at being the insufferable nuisance that others have been to us.

Before we were old enough to know better, someone usually was handy when the diaper reached critical-mass stage or the second teeth begged an orthodontic consultation. We noticed no more that the latter forced parents to pinch the budget than that the former made them pinch their noses.

Instead, we went our merry way, thinking Pampers and braces were part of the hospital goody kit presented to new moms as they were sent home with their swaddled infants.

Such is the innocence of children; such are the preoccupations of adolescence.

We usually don't catch a blindsided swat at the head for our thoughtlessness until we make a sharp right turn at the street marked Adulthood.

If we could remember at that juncture that one day we will get to wear plaid, the idea might help us through some of the lesser annoyances of playing "taxi-mom" or coaching the T-ball team that God forgot.

When I am an old man I'll wear plaid and a pink tie with a hula girl that wiggles when I walk.

When a youngster (growing too old to use that as an excuse anymore) wants to use the carefully budgeted tuition money on rock-climbing lessons in New Mexico, it is a good time to remember Casey's poem:

I shall spend my children's inheritance on fast horses, fast cars and slow women, and I will say I have no money for birthday gifts. I will turn the TV on as loudly as I want and watch football games in my boxer shorts.

Hmm.

So on we go through life, entering the job market and trying to strike a fair contract between what we think we're worth and what the market will bear.

Sometimes we get lucky: Some bosses never seem to notice that we're there. Some never take their eyes off us. A happy medium is a blessing to all.

About the time our Social Security card starts to get dog-eared enough to be put to good use, plaid starts to look really good.

Even the neighborhood gossip begins to show signs of having redeeming value. There is something deliciously tantalizing about the thought of knocking on his or her door (for gossip surely is a gender-neutral avocation) with dentures out, Speedo on, promising, "You'll probably be seeing a lot more of me now that I'm retired."

Who knows? Maybe we'll get our picture in the neighborhood association's newsletter.

And won't it just be wonderful to stroll into a fast-food restaurant, pick the surliest-looking 18-year-old behind the counter and announce, "I chose you because you remind me of the nephew whose birthday I always remembered even when he forgot mine. I stopped sending him wedding gifts after the third marriage. With any kind of luck, he's in prison. But, just so you learn early to count your blessing, I've brought my bowling team along for lunch, and we want separate checks. Here are the coupons and the Golden Buckeye cards."

Oh, yeah. We're going to like plaid a lot. And, if we're smart, we'll buy a pair of outrageously baggy, lime-colored shorts to match.

That way, when we walk along the beach with our metal detector at sunset, interrupting young lovers with too many glands and too little spandex, they'll have a good description to give the beach patrol after we bonk them on the head with our metal detector and remind them, "Thou, too, art mortal."

Mister Thoreau's Pond

May 5, 1993

I am of the mind that a modicum of the popularity of outdoor clothiers L.L. Bean and Lands' End can be traced to that faint desire yet flickering in humankind's breast to turn our backs on the "quiet desperation" of our lives today and find -- as did Thoreau -- our Walden Pond.

Sadly, what we seem to seek is not a shoe substantial enough in which to march to unconventional cadences but rather a hiking boot sufficiently stylish to wear to the cocktail reception for the opening of a new gallery.

Thoreau, whose death anniversary Thursday will go little noticed, would have laughed at our folly. A man who lived by the motto "Beware of all enterprises that require new clothes" could not have helped smiling at a generation that needs not even the pretense of enterprise to reach for the MasterCard.

Our mistake in pondering Thoreau's life is to come away with the conclusion that its message urged us to drop out. Not so. It was, rather, to drop in. He wasn't telling us to get out of our condos so much as to get into our heads.

He wrote, "I went to the woods because I wished to live deliberately, to front only the essential facts of life, and see if I could not learn what it had come to teach and not, when I came to die, discover that I had not lived."

It was not for the song of the whippoorwill or the comforting croak of frogs at nightfall that he left the nearby town of Concord, Mass.

The stock journalistic sop to Thoreau's Walden Pond is the piece written or narrated by some conscience-smitten scribe bemoaning the rape of the environment, the tragedy of paving paradises that could better be used for silent meditation.

Save the tears. The problem is not that we don't have anyplace for would-be Thoreaus to meditate; it is that we don't have any would-be Thoreaus.

Thoreau didn't need a pond. He could have gone to Columbus City Center every day for two years and faced no greater distraction than accidentally sitting on a cinnamon roll the size of a cow's head.

The setting is incidental to the undertaking: *Walden* could just as easily have been called Kings Island.

We don't have the gumption to do what Thoreau did. We have car payments and house payments and a Saturday morning tee time.

Even if we could, we have spent so much time rolling down the narrow confines of our career paths that we not only lack the breadth of mind to distinguish the forest from the trees but also can't see the trees anymore.

We may talk about needing more personal space -- time to get to know ourselves and reflect, to smell the roses. For too many of us, though, it takes only a three-hour power failure to realize the lie in such wistful longing.

We eat, belch, go to work, watch the tube, go to bed and start all over again. Our minds remain vast primordial swamps that not only go unchartered but may as well intimidate the faint.

Several days ago, I heard a stranger guffaw, "My mind is a neighborhood in which I wouldn't want to be caught alone after dark."

That is truly sad - because the book written by the man who died 131 years ago Thursday is all we need as a compass for those unexplored reaches.

"It is an invitation to life's dance," E.B. White praised.

Having danced that dance, Thoreau, when fate forced him to confront his mortality at the tender age of 44, was able to do it with sublime acceptance.

"Henry, have you made your peace with God?" he was asked by an aunt as he lay on his deathbed.

Thoreau said that he didn't believe he and God had ever quarreled.

The measure of such a man and the desire to strive toward his height are both lost upon today's society.

We don't want to go to Walden. We just want the L.L. Bean parka that makes us look as if we might have thought about it once upon a time.

Homo Sapiens In the Military

April 18, 1993

My Dear Nephew Mike,

I could spend half a day chewing the fat about the goings-on in your little hometown of Methane. Fact is, Nothing much is new around here since last I took pen in hand, except for Iny Rae Nutter's crusade.

I could tell you about it, but the letter she has been sending to every soul in town sort of says it all:

Dear Friend,

We've got trouble here in this wonderful little country of yours and mine, and I don't have to tell you what it is.

Us good country people here in Methane are used to calling a spade a spade. But, just so nobody thinks I'm being crude, I won't use the word the fellas use down at the gas station to discuss this problem. I'll use that other 50-cent word.

You know what I'm talking about. I'm talking about Homo sapiens. I'm talking about letting Homo sapiens wear the proud uniform of the arm services of the good old U.S. of A.

I've heard what the other side has to say: This is 1993. Live and let live. They can't help it if they were born Homo sapiens. They're just like us.

I tell you: That is part of the problem. Used to be that you could walk in a restaurant or supermarket and spot a Homo sapien a mile away. Now you can't tell anymore. There's Homo sapien teachers and ministers. Five years I've been going to the same doctor for my bursitis and never had the slightest idea he was a Homo sapien.

They're even in government, politics. I think half the problem with Washington is that Congress is run by a bunch of Homo sapiens.

But the military? That's where I draw the line.

Now all of you know that there is a statue in the town square dedicated to my great-grandfather, Augustus Gamaliel Nutter. Not many people remember it these days, but with 300 Union soldiers - most of them green and right off the farm -- he took on 8,000 Rebels led by Stonewall Jackson. Of course he didn't win. Only 83 of his men were standing when it was over. Yes, he was outnumbered. No way he could have done it. But I'll bet you can't name one Homo sapien who would have tried the same thing.

People just don't understand that sometimes you've got to make tough decisions in war. Take that Lt. Calley in Vietnam. They raked him over the coals because of what he did. Some Homo sapiens would have probably said, "Now wait a minute here. Maybe all these people ain't the enemy." And how would Vietnam have turned out if we had done that?

I shudder to think what my great-granddaddy would be saying about this problem we got today.

Everyone is looking at the big picture. I say just to look at the day-to-day things. Would you or your spouse want a Homo sapien sleeping close enough to you that you could hear him snore? Would you want a Homo sapien watching you get dressed in the morning?

The military can't give everybody separate rooms. Lord, when they sign up troops, they might throw 250 naked guys in the same room for a physical. You could look all around, and you wouldn't have a clue in the world that some of them were Homo sapiens unless they came right out and told you.

You see, even though the military ain't to blame, they make the problem even worse. They shave everyone's head and give everyone the same uniform, and pretty soon everyone looks exactly the same. You get them on the rifle range or the obstacle course, and you don't know the Homo sapiens from the rest. You could take them into battle and say, "I need three soldiers to volunteer to go take out that sniper," and they could all be Homo sapiens.

No, you just can't let them in the service. It's gotten so hard out here in civilian life that you can't even spot them anymore unless they're carrying protest signs. Get them in uniform, and we'll never be able to tell.

Think about it.

Sincerely,

Iny Rae Nutter

Well, Mike, I guess that's about all the news you need from Methane, so I'll close for now.

My best to your momma.

Love,

Aunt Gracie

Reflections on an Average Sunrise

April 14, 1993

At 6:55 this morning, if the sun was visible to the awakening minister, he glimpsed in its presence a metaphor for his homily on the everlasting wonder of the constancy of God's promises.

The astronomer, gaze fixed on the eastern horizon, saw a commonplace dwarf star composed largely of helium and hydrogen, perhaps the ashes of its predecessors. Interesting but hardly remarkable.

To the aspiring poet, the sunrise was a welcome allusion for the radiance of his true love's face. The sun, of course, places a poor second to his true love's face and likely rhymes with "fun."

Buoyed by an auspicious spring beginning for hay, the farmer saw in today's rising sun a chance to get out in the fields and plant corn, perhaps soybeans. Some of the sweet corn is already in the ground.

The American Indian saw in the sun the god that his ancestors had feared, revered and beseeched with their supplications. The old ones speak of those who lanced their chest muscles with skewers and tethered themselves to the ceremonial cottonwood for the sun dance. This they did until the white man forbade it as barbaric. The white man.

In pondering the celestial event that marked the end of her shift, the night-duty hospice nurse gazed upon something that one of her patients would never again see. Funny, the things we take for granted.

The defendant saw it as the dawning of a day whose end would be marked by celebration or incarceration.

The inmate saw it as day No. 857.

The optimist saw it as the beginning of a partly sunny day; the pessimist, the start of a partly cloudy day.

The environmentalist saw it as the summons to a day in which a wasteful America would continue to throw its non-biodegradable rubbish into non-biodegradable sacks for a burial in land growing ever more scarce.

To the trash man, it looked like eight more hours of steady work.

The convenience-store clerk viewed it as his good-luck charm. When he's around to see it rise, the worst part of his day is over.

Refracted through the windshield of her car on the way to school, the English teacher saw the sunrise as the precursor of a day in which she would once more try to make 24 seniors understand that Hemingway's *The Old Man and the Sea* is actually an odyssey of Faustian self-discovery. Twenty-four seniors would see it as a fish story and remind themselves that the rising sun was proof sufficient that only 37 more days of high school remained.

To the family practitioner, the sun looked like two upper-respiratory infections, four cases of viral gastroenteritis, one possible diverticulitis, one plantar wart and a pair of hypochondriacs.

No matter how shaded by clouds, the sun at 6:55 would have been just a little too bright to a wino. Nothing, though, that a half a fifth of Wild Irish Rose couldn't soften.

A homicide detective looks at the sun a bit differently. It's ray forever betray what the incautious killer left in haste the night before: bodies in Dumpsters, victims in the weeds.

To those who believe in such things, the sun ushered in a day in which Leos will see matters of the heart take on a new glow. Sagittarians might find it a rocky day for money matters. Those born under the sign of Cancer will find that chatting with relatives could reveal untapped financial resources. Maybe.

The sun rose on the 104th day of 1993, and no two people regarded it in precisely the same way. Some saw it as a chance to begin anew. Some looked at it, drew the blinds and went back to sleep.

Only the child marveled, "Wow!"

The Artist

March 28, 1993

He held a pencil the way one might grip a spent tube of Crest, squeezing for an elusive last dollop of fluoride goodness to deposit on the bristles of a poised brush.

I, the subject of his labored sketching, dared not budge from my seat at the dining room table. Knuckles curled beneath my chin as if mocking the sculptor Rodin's most famous work, I sat frozen, the artist's reluctant model.

We doting parents spare the landfill the creations issued from the innocent paws of our offspring. Such minor masterpieces are the paper currency that they deposit for approval and attention, and that we hoard for the imminent rainy day when they have outgrown the need for such transactions before we have. Their small investments mature at a surprisingly swift rate.

When a child is both contemplative and roguish, a parent finds it tough to guess whether the presidency or prison would best showcase his natural inclinations.

Aaron has always been that way.

In his moments of introspection, he bore the earnest look of a cryptographer trying to unscramble the cipher of the muse. At play, he had a daredevil inventiveness that seemed to have no purpose beyond providing emergency-room orderlies with a string of incredible anecdotes to pass along in the hospital cafeteria.

The sutured remembrances of his childhood calamities he treated with the affectionate reverence that a German cavalry officer might have for a dueling scar earned at Heidelberg.

Still, he was ever the artist.

One of the few times I cannot recall seeing him with a sketchbook under his arm was the time yet another intern was refining the seamstress's craft on a lacerated part of Aaron's anatomy.

It is a sad truth, but the artistic inclination of many children diminishes about the same time they outgrow their fascination with imperial storm troopers or mutant turtles.

Those who stick with it seem as often driven by it as enchanted. Through its evolution, talent seeks outlets that often confound fogies who cannot understand why it would be squandered, painting concert banners for a heavy-metal garage band, when it could be employed to create salable still lifes.

When Aaron was most vulnerable to being lured by peer pressure from the self-discipline that his gift demands, a persistent high-school art teacher named Art Counts stepped in to alternately praise and cuff him as necessity dictated. The teacher dogged his aspirant to finish a comprehensive portfolio for scholarship consideration a few months ago, when any 18-year-old in his right mind was supposed to be letting it all hang out over Christmas break.

For a while he disappeared, cloistering himself in his room at his art table like some mad, hellbent scrivener.

When all was finished and matted, he carried it to the powers that be at the Columbus College of Art and Design.

While he waited, he fretted over the choices he had submitted. I reminded him that artists' continual need to be reassured is what keeps them from becoming loan officers. He took small comfort.

We subject our talent to scrutiny from above with the same trepidation that might be demonstrated by a worshiper who has no blood sacrifice to lay on the altar of an avenging god except a pet rodent that died of prosaic causes.

For days, Aaron trudged out to the mailbox in expectation, only to return to the house empty-handed.

When good news first made its way around school, it was that a fellow student had won a $16,000 scholarship.

At times, sympathy smacks too much of patronization. Sometimes we can't help our children. We can only hurt for them.

I was lost in thought when I picked up the telephone the next day and heard him tell me he had won an $18,000 scholarship to help him practice art.

Somewhere -- I know it's on one of the closet shelves -- I have that sketch he drew of me when he was 5. I knew all along, of course, that he was going to do it. I'd tell anyone who would listen, if I could swallow right now.

Telephone Tree

March 12, 1993

Of the trees I tended when my offspring were mere children, I recall most the one of least arboreal authenticity -- a nuisance network of baby boomers-turned-parents we came to call the "telephone tree."

Hooked into it, we were the French resistance of the "burbs," a fearsome band of Volvo-driving, child-doting, petition-waving, permanent-press anarchists bristling to do battle with school boards, mayors, township trustees, Japanese beetles.

It didn't take much to set us off. The rumor of a school levy or the scent of uncollected garbage sent us scrambling for the phones to marshall the militia.

Our fingers walked, as well, for matters of far less consequence. We were forever on the phone with the parents of right and left fielders, relaying word of Little League rainouts or makeup games. Ma Bell was our collective recourse when Mother Nature wrecked plans for our children's religious-education classes or PTA meetings.

Somewhere within the recesses of my brainpan exists the echo of a host of familiar phone voices with which I could not possibly begin to match faces.

The children grew. The telephone tree, accordingly, shed that which was no longer vital to emergencies great and small. Adolescents establish their own communications networks.

There is now but one stubborn leaf left tenaciously holding on the high reaches of the boughs. It is a telephone tree that was started a few years before my first child was born.

Age, fate and military obligations conspired to assemble a curious congregation of rebels, malcontents and not a few serious cases of arrested development.

Had we been civilians, many of us would have been hanging around Haight-Asbury trying to conform to the norms of non-conformity. But all our bell-bottoms were government issue, all our marching was done to the beat of an indifferent drummer.

We said goodbye to one another at Bethesda Naval Hospital in 1968.

Joe, J.V., Tim, Tom, Andy and Jim left for Vietnam first. Jerry pulled duty on a hospital ship. Jack had already pulled his tour earlier and seen more action than any of us cared to know about. The rest of us waited on the inevitable orders to Southeast Asia.

Charlie stayed behind to make sure our payroll records arrived in Da Nang the same time we did. Ironically, Janine, one of the most able medical hands among us, stayed put at Bethesda because the Navy was not sending women into combat with Marine ground units.

We all made it safely home, put away our uniforms and promised one another that our circle would always remain unbroken. We had one another and our telephone tree to keep abreast of marriages, babies, divorces -- the works.

Ten years ago we had our first reunion, not far from the old hospital. Two were no longer among us. We lost one to heart disease, another to suicide.

As we had earlier, we vowed to stay in touch. We, after all, had our marvelous telephone tree.

Two of our group faced heart problems during the past year. One required surgery; the other soon may.

One night last week the telephone tree jangled to life with fresh news that Jack had lung cancer. His prospects were predictably grim; the disease already had spread.

After I got over the initial shock, I was to call two more friends and let them know.

Charlie, in Virginia, handled it well. I was worried about having to tell Janine. We had always teased Jack and Janine about being madly in love, and though they threw scant evidence our way that would hold up in court, something smoldered there.

To my surprise, Janine, who lives in Tucson, Ariz., took the news in stride. I understood why when I inquired about her health. She had faced not one mastectomy but two.

"We're getting older," she said.

What she meant was, "We're not invincible."

With typical wryness, she reminded me, "I'll be 46 on April Fools' Day. Come to my party. The secret passwords are, 'Yeah, Janine, I got you a gift.'"

I wished her well.

The telephone tree was silent. A capricious wind tugs at a leaf here and there, dangerously twisting the stem that holds it to the branch.

We watch and wait, hoping the phone doesn't ring.

The Great Wall of Graffiti

January 13, 1993

The Great Wall of Graffiti went up during the holidays.

Paint, wallpaper or paneling would have been more practical, but such *Better Home & Gardens* notions about decorating often escape 18-year-old high-school seniors.

To create a graffiti wall was not the first unconventional interior-design decision made by my daughter, Annie.

Two years ago, tired of flat latex peach, she decided that the walls should be painted white, then dappled with black enamel paint flung from a trim brush while standing in the middle of the room. She liked the effect -- which I called nouveau vandalism.

But adolescent tastes are fickle, and, when boredom recently overtook her, she decided that the spatter motif had to go to make way for graffiti.

Being the typical parent, I was concerned, at first, that my daughter's bedroom soon would bear a striking resemblance to a restroom at a campus-area bar.

Word went out quickly about the graffiti wall, and there was no shortage of visitors bearing felt-tip pens.

"Hopes can only go up. Tears can only go down," wrote one scribe, attributing the quotation to "Blues Traveler."

One writer, quoting the Rolling Stones, scribbled, "You can't always get what you want, but sometimes you get what you need."

Some of the quotations are morose, brooding, pessimistic about life. Some sing anthems to life's sweeter moments.

A quotation from Shelley offers:

I can give not what men call love,
But wilt thou accept not the worship the heart lifts above
And the heavens reject not,
The desire of
the month for the star,
Of the night for the morrow.

Not unexpectedly, some of the quotations are openly rebellious.

"The truest form of democracy is anarchy," wrote a friend of Annie's who signed the message simply "B.A."

A few of the etchings pose questions steeped in irony. One writer, quoting Lily Tomlin, asks, "Why is it when you talk to God you're praying, but when God talks to you you're schizophrenic?"

One afternoon while my daughter was in school, I sat in her room and studied her proud creation. The quotations reminded me of nothing so much as how acutely, in adolescence, we sense the broad sweep of human emotion: love, sorrow, hate, passion and awe.

Like a bird on a wire,
Like a drunk in a midnight choir.
I have tried, in my way, to be free.

Leonard Cohen wrote that a quarter-century ago, but for some reason it has had staying power.

Not all of Annie's friends thought the graffiti wall was a good idea. Near the edge of one of her windows, I read, "Leaving quotes on this wall would be narrow-minded."

But most of the quotations, if not always verbatim, are thoughtful, reflective:

"Love is so short. Forgetting is so long."

"And in the depths of my darkest winter, I found within my soul an invincible summer."

"You write a quote," Annie had suggested, stuffing a pen in my hand.

Writing something typically parental in tone, I penned, "You can never begin to understand the universe until you realize you are not the center of it."

She studied that quotation only a few moments before penning one of her own:

"How can you ask me to speak my heart about Vietnam when my heart is still there?"

That message she signed not with her American name but with the name she was given at birth: Thanh Tuyen Nguyen. Beneath that, in parentheses, she wrote, "Ahm Chung Em," Vietnamese for "I love you."

Sitting on the edge of my daughter's bed, transcribing wall inscriptions, I realized that the day was growing long, that she soon would be home from school to reclaim her room.

"This wall was started by Annie Harden, Adam Burdette and Braden McClung," I read.

Too soon, Annie will be getting on with life on her own. I was reminded anew of that inevitable reality when I glimpsed, among the quotations on the wall, the last words of Oscar Wilde:

"This wallpaper is killing me. One of us has got to go."

Annie

November 23, 1992

Happy birthday, kiddo.

We won't light candles or sing the birthday dirge, purely for the sake of sparing you a musical tribute that your invited friends might think childish or geeky.

Here's a check.

I suppose that children have come of age when maturity convinces them of their parents' ineptness at picking gifts. Money is the gift that keeps on giving.

Somewhere northwest of Saigon - forgive me; we now call it Ho Chi Minh City -- is a hamlet known as Bien Hiep.

For all of your 18 years, I have tried to learn more about it, with little success.

You were born there to a mother about whom I know little and into circumstances about which I know less.

You were scarcely 5 weeks old when your mother carried you from the hamlet to Vinh Long Orphanage, depositing you in the care of the nuns on the day after Christmas 1974.

Sickly from the start, you developed spinal meningitis on the "Babylift" flight to the United States.

The doctors at Letterman Army Hospital in San Francisco had little hope that you would pull through.

You toughed that one out, your head shaved (years before Sinead O'Connor made it vogue) to accommodate the intravenous lines.

No more than knee-high when you became a U.S. citizen, you nonetheless lifted your arm and swore your allegiance to the country of your adoption.

Your mom and I, and certainly your brothers, tried to shield you from the slurs that followed your arrival. Your older brother lost a childhood playmate because of a parent who did not want his boy associating with "them."

I know little about the well from which you draw your inner strength. It was sufficient to earn you a spot as catcher in a predominantly boys' sport, cheerleader in a predominantly white-bread high school.

I was on the sidelines recently when you quarterbacked your fellow seniors to victory over a spirited junior team. For the sake of space, we will not talk of interceptions.

So now you have come of age. You are old enough to vote for those who run this country, old enough to go off and fight their wars.

Like the groaning board of a banquet table, your life is spread before you now. The mailbox is routinely filled with invitations from colleges. It is hard to get a word in edgewise on your answering machine for all the friends who routinely call seeking your presence at this gathering or that.

Somehow, you made it from diapers to proms without being scarred by the taunts of those who thought you "ought to go back where you came from."

The night before your 18th birthday, I arrived home to find you at the dining room table, working on an editorial about racism for your high school newspaper.

Your treatise was half-finished, yet you were only half-satisfied with the results. You wanted your readers to understand the hurt and brutality that can be leveled by a single word.

"If you want to make the point," I advised, "why don't you use the same words that bigots use to try to diminish you?"

You pondered that suggestion for a while, arguing that such strong language might not make it past your journalism advisor.

When such strong language is used as an appeal to end racism, I contended, it can be even stronger than when it is employed to perpetuate it.

In the end, you relented.

Together we tried to think of every racial or ethnic slur.

"How do you spell 'nigger'?" you asked, penning your reasons it should never be used to describe a person of color.

Nothing makes me prouder than knowing you made it to 18 without knowing how to spell that word.

Nothing hurts more than knowing that you long ago were made aware of how to spell "gook."

The Old Man's Son

August 12, 1992

I get a little moody each year on this day, a bit pensive and preoccupied. Nothing clinical about it. Around dusk I'll head to the back deck and talk to the dog about it, and I'll be all right.

You see, today is the old man's birthday, and there's no old man to celebrate it with.

A heart attack took him 14 years ago.

It makes me downright envious sometimes when I overhear people talking about their fathers - especially fathers still living robust and busy lives at 80 or 90.

The old man made it to only 54.

Tucked away in the family room is a small cache of photographs. His mother, who outlived him by several years, made me a small present of the pictures not long before we carried her up the old hill near

Haydenville and lowered her into a grave next to dozens of family head-stones, which she had been visiting since she was a girl. She's right next to her husband and not much farther than an arm's length from her boy.

Her boy.

She was especially fond of a photograph of him at 12 or 13. Wearing bib overalls, his hair slicked back with Brilliantine, he had recently recovered from a bout with rheumatic fever.

I don't think I ever saw him looking more carefree than he does in a black-and-white snapshot in which he is leaning against the sea wall in Corpus Christi, Texas; it was the summer of '42. He is wearing his Navy uniform, and his hat is cocked in a defiant sort of way.

The war was on, and he was itching to get aboard a ship. He was willing to do almost anything for that chance and was certain the Navy wouldn't make him spend the entire war showing films about venereal disease to new arrivals at the Corpus Christi Naval Air Station.

A few months after that snapshot was taken, he contracted a flulike virus. The doctor who treated him detected the heart murmur he had managed to sneak past the draft board. He suddenly found himself a civilian again.

I don't think he ever forgave the Navy, although, when he died, the copy of *The Bluejackets' Manual* he was issued in boot camp was still in his top dresser drawer.

There is a picture of the old man and me, fishing along the banks of the Muskingum River. I am 4 and seem to be having a terrible time. Shirtless and seated next to me, my father is looking at something across the river.

He was a Buick man. Automobile allegiance was a big thing to men of his generation. Thus, it is only natural that in one photo he stands proudly at the side of a vintage road boat. It looks to be a '54 Roadmaster.

When he turned 50, we surprised him with a party, showing up at his Grove City mobile home after he had convinced himself that it was unlikely that any of his six offspring had remembered the significance of the day.

Seated in his favorite chair, holding the cake we had taken him, he seems in pain. The smile is forced.

The hardest picture to look at is one in which he proudly holds aloft my oldest son -- who was 4 at the time -- the last time the three of us went fishing together.

The last time I spoke to my father, it was in anger. Bullheaded and ever independent, he had decided that he no longer needed the heart medication that doctors had prescribed.

He endured my scolding in silence. The goodbye he tendered at the end of my tirade was the last word I heard him speak.

Now and again I'll run into acquaintances who are at odds with their fathers.

"Make your peace while there is still time," I always urge.

That way you won't have to deal with that lump of remorse and unconveyed love that catches in the throat while you look at a handful of pictures on a certain significant day.

And you won't have to talk to the dog.

Politically Correct

July 24, 1992

I made a saddening discovery the other day while leafing through my newly purchased copy of the Henry Beard and Christopher Cerf book, *The Official Politically Correct Dictionary and Handbook.*

While it is possible that this volume (by two living white males) may teach me a thing or two about gender-neutral writing, if I live by its prescription for political correctness, I am going to have to change all of the songs I know.

John Denver's *Lady,* for instance, will have to changed. It will have to be Womyn, Womon or Womban, according to Beard and Cerf. "Lady" is sexist.

I suppose that also means John Lennon's *Woman* will have to be changed to delete the incorrect gender-ender "man."

Forget Gary Puckett's *Young Girl.* "Girl" has been replaced with "prewoman," as in:

Prewoman, get out of my life.
My love for you is way out of line.
Better run, prewoman,
You're much too young, prewoman.

Puckett also will have to change *This Girl Is a Woman Now.* It will become This Prewoman Is a Womban Now.

Roger Miller's *Husbands and Wives* is a neat little song. But "wife" is now "significant other," "unpaid sex worker" or "domestic incarceration survivor."

That also means that anyone who wants to do a politically correct version of one of the late Marty Robbins' greatest hits will sing My Womban, My Womban, My Domestic Incarceration Survivor.

When I was a child, I got a kick out of Patti Page's *How Much Is That Doggie in the Window.* But a dog is now a "non-human animal companion." Let us sing:

How much is that non-human animal companion in the window?
The one with the waggly tail.
How much is that non-human animal companion in the window?
I do hope that non-human animal companion's for sale.

Cerf and Beard wonder whether changing "dog" to "animal companion" also will mean changing "pet rock" to "mineral companion."

Remember Rufus Thomas and *Do the Funky Chicken*? Because a chicken is considered by some groups a "voiceless victim of speciesism," that little must be changed to Do the Funky Voiceless Victim of Speciesism.

A rose is a rose is a rose, right?

No, a rose is a "botanical companion." to be more specific, it is a "multi-petaled, soilistically challenged, botanical companion."

Vic Dana would have to croon:

I want some red multi-petaled, soilistically challenged, botanical companions.

For a blue womban.

Pity James Brown. *Prisoner of Love* will become the more politically correct Client of the Correctional System of Love.

Because of sanctions against "heightism," one of Annette Funicello's greatest hits will have to be modified to Vertically Different Paul.

If "tall" is taboo, so is "short," as well as "fat." A short person is "vertically constrained." A fat person is a "person of size." Thus, singer Larry Williams' *Short Fat Fannie* will become Vertically Constrained, Person of Size Fannie.

In some cases, even the name of the performer must be changed. The artist who sang the 1956 hit *Blueberry Hill* will have to be called "Person of Size" Domino.

From reading Cerf and Beard, I find it difficult to tell where they stand on the whole political correctness movement. However, they include in the book the following quotation from George Orwell's *1984*:

"It was intended that when Newspeak had been adopted once and for all and Oldspeak forgotten, a heretical thought...should be literally unthinkable, at least so far as thought is dependent on words."

Cerf and Beard dedicate the book to Donna Ellen Cooperman, "who, after a courageous yearlong battle through the New York state court system, won the right to be known as Donna Ellen Cooperperson."

The Town That Wouldn't Die

June 11, 1992

YOUGHIOGHENY LAKE, Pa. - Small towns often die so slowly that we scarcely notice their passing until they are gone.

A factory or a mill shuts down; a coal seam is played out. The young flee in search of fortune elsewhere. The old hang on. Another community dies of natural causes.

But at Youghiogheny Lake, I found a town summarily executed by the U.S. government. The only problem is that it refuses to stay buried.

John "Capt. Jack" Cornish, 73, is said to be the last surviving resident of Somerfield, Pa. The son of the innkeeper of the Cornish Arms, he came of age listening to old-timers recall the rich history of the area.

George Washington passed through the valley that cradled Somerfield several times, putting up at an old inn called Spier's Tavern. In 1818, President James Monroe and an entourage from Washington officially opened the stone bridge that spanned the Youghiogheny River and carried Rt. 40, the National Road, through Somerfield.

President William McKinley for several years spent part of his summers at the Cornish Arms.

Then, in 1936, after floods ravaged parts of western Pennsylvania and Ohio, the federal government decided to dam the Youghiogheny. Doing so would create a lake that would wind for 16 miles and submerge Somerfield.

The project did not set well with the 150 families who called Somerfield home. Among the most strident opponents was a 90-year-old former state senator named James Endsley.

"He said they would have to carry him out. He would not leave," Cornish remembered. Endsley and his wife died in Somerfield just before the clearing and demolition began.

The houses and churches, the grocery and the bank all went quickly.

"The government tore them down," Cornish said. "Then they cut down every tree. There was nothing left standing taller than 3 feet." Two cemeteries were relocated on higher ground.

As for the Cornish Arms, the family was able to save a few souvenirs: the mantel, a few pillars from the side porch, the lamp that crowned the entrance.

Cornish was away in the Army in 1942 when all traces of Somerfield, save one, were submerged. A large white house on a ridge above the Youghiogheny was spared. Cornish eventually bought it.

When life deals you lemons, make lemonade. When the government covers your house with a lake, build a marina. That is how Cornish came to be called "Capt. Jack." The driveway that stretches in front of his marina once was the National Road.

When the government finished its business, Cornish was sure he had seen the last of Somerfield. Not so. During droughts, the bridge that Monroe had dedicated was visible above the water, just down the slope from the marina.

It was a sight that drew gawkers from far and wide. Drivers on nearby Rt. 40 often spied it and turned around, unable to continue along the National Road until they had asked a local why there was a bridge in Youghiogheny Lake.

Then, last autumn, when the weather's caprice and the demand for drinking water by downstream municipalities conspired to lower the lake more than usual, a peculiar thing happened.

Not only did the bridge appear, but building foundations also became visible, along with sidewalks on which Cornish had played as a child.

The lake's deepest spot is normally 125 feet. In the fall it was half that.

Cornish witnessed the outline of Somerfield reappearing, the foundations of the bank and the grocery -- and, yes, the Cornish Arms.

"Makes you feel sad," he acknowledged. "I had a lot of happy days down there before it was covered up."

The front porch of Somerfield's lone surviving house used to afford Cornish a fine view of the lake, but two spruces have grown so tall they now obscure it.

I doubt that makes Cornish unhappy.

The Fields of Antietam

June 10, 1992

SHARPSBURG, Md. - Upon a road once littered with the Civil War dead and now marked with yard-sale signs, the soft rains of early summer spattered the two-lane highway. It was as if tears were being shed upon the disparity separating yesterday's epic sorrow from today's urge to turn a dollar on a slightly used lava lamp.

One must trudge through knee-high foxtail to reach the heart of the story, but it is there, etched into an obelisk of stone on a now-pastoral field, where North and South fought the bloodiest battle of the Civil War.

At the foot of a monument crowned with the name of my native state, a simple inscription recalls, "In this field Ohio's sons sacrificed life and health for the country and one flag."

On a day in mid-September 130 years ago, 87,000 Union troops faced the bold northward incursion of 40,000 Southerners. Before the sun set on their battle, 23,110 American soldiers had been killed or wounded.

The heroic Civil War nurse Clara Barton found it necessary, according to one account, to pause routinely during her ministrations that day to wring blood from her skirt hems. It has been chronicled that, along a stretch of ground near Antietam Creek called Sunken Road, it was possible to walk yard upon yard of the lines of engagement without touching the ground. The turf had been sodded unbroken with corpses.

So, once a year, the good folks of Sharpsburg marshal bands and color guard, lift salute rifles and fashion wreaths in homage to their sad notoriety.

Amid the Saturday drizzle attending this year's ceremony, a band perched upon the front porch of the town's funeral home played *Dixie* and *When Johnny Comes Marching Home*, for a crowd milling around vendors selling hot dogs to benefit the Little League or souvenir balloons to benefit themselves.

Incongruity sprouted like quick grass along Sharpsburg's main thoroughfare. A middle-aged man, clad in the Union garb of Pennsylvania's 105th Regimental Band, held a minicam against his shoulder to capture his fellow musicians in repose before the ceremonies.

In the shadow of the high wall of a stone house that remains pocked with cannon fire, dignitaries paused to honor the dead of Antietam.

Within that house, beneath the polished replacement flooring, rest timbers that still carry the bloodstains of the wounded carried in after Antietam's storm.

There but for the timidity of commanding Union Gen. George McClellan, the back of the Confederacy might have been broken in 1862. He could have pushed into the Potomac River the battle-ravaged and retreating soldiers of Gen. Robert E. Lee and, some think, hastened the end of the Civil War. For that and other sins of reluctance, Lincoln relieved McClellan of his command of Union forces two months after he had repulsed the Confederates at Sharpsburg.

While hot dogs sizzled, Sno-Kones chilled and children frolicked on the sidewalks of Sharpsburg, 4,776 Union victims lay beneath grave grass on the fringe of town.

Historian Geoffrey Ward recorded that Confederates under Lee's command marched into town singing *Maryland, My Maryland*, hoping to win the fickle favor of a state of divided allegiance. They retreated carrying south their wounded in a wagon train that, some say, stretched 17 miles.

Headed in the opposite direction, pondering such huge sacrifice, we nosed the rental car toward Rt. 40.

We passed the battlefield where, each year just before Christmas, luminarias equal to the 23,110 casualties are set out to light the December sky.

Upon that gently sloping field, a nation once attempted suicide. It survived, but, if the blood tribute exacted as toll could not be sponged by mourners' tears, it surely will not be erased by Sharpsburg's annual commemoration or the rains of a millennium of early summers upon the fields of Antietam.

"Someone's Always Leaving"

November 6, 1988

Just outside of Richmond, Va. I switched the car radio from rock to country. Debra, I thought, was asleep, and Bon Jovi was beginning to seem like Chinese water torture. It took but two verses of a real country bleeder called *Blue to the Bone* to stir my wife from slumber.

"How come someone's always leaving?" she asked.

"If no one ever left," I explained, "the Country Music Association awards would be about three and a half minutes long."

She doesn't understand country, but I'm working on it. Until she married me, her idea of country was, say, someone like Jimmy Dickens singing *Take an Old Cold 'Tater and Wait* to an audience of toothless Ma and Pa Kettle yahoos.

"Country has changed" I tell her, speaking as one who's earliest childhood memory is of a huge crackling Philco radio tuned to WSM and Grand Ol' Opry every Saturday night. "They don't all sing through their noses and drive around in Cadillac convertibles with longhorn hood ornaments."

Unfortunately, just when it seems I have her convinced that country music is more sophisticated than she thinks, I flip on the tube to confront some character with opposums embroidered on his orange leisure suit doing a musical lament about the day his best coon dog drowned in the septic tank.

We were watching a Nashville Network program several days ago when who should appear but Minnie Pearl. Debra took one look at Minnie and shook her head in disbelief.

"She's always dressed that way," I explained. Minnie was wearing one of her trademark dresses, a dress that would have looked better on curtain rods at an east Tennessee truckstop. Resting upon her head was a hat -- Carmen Miranda would have wept -- adorned with 27 varieties of wax fruit, a half dozen Hummels and the clutch assembly from a Ford Bronco. The price tag, as ever, dangled by a string from the hat brim.

"Minnie's a good ol' girl," I defended. "She does a lot fine work for charity and stuff."

Debra shrugged.

I have given up trying to apologize to her for the rhyme scheme country singers occasionally use, wincing each time Loretta Lynn warbles:

The work we done was hard,

At night we'd sleep cause we were tard.

By now, Debra knows that what "skips a beat" when "you walk down the street" is not Buck Owens' heart, rather his "hort."

It strikes her as strange that Grammy Award winners will often thank "my personal Lord and Savior Jesus Christ" for giving them the talent to write a song about cheating, lying and boozing it up.

"And leaving," she interjects.

She thinks there is a lot of sexism in country lyrics. I tell her that it is changing. I tell that women are no longer portrayed as mere sex objects in most country music today.

"They don't call them puddin' or darlin' anymore," I protest, usually 30 seconds before Mel McDaniel sings *Baby's Got Her Blue Jeans On* or Buck Owens asked the Musical question:

Has anybody here seen sweet thang?

I doubt that she will ever be able to handle serious bluegrass music. The high pitched, and often mournful, nasality of it is a bit much for her. Too, bluegrass songs often go on interminably. It is not enough that the spurned suitor stabs his former lover. He has to think about it first for six verses. Another two or three verses are consumed by the trip to the house-wares section of a discount store to pick out something with a good sharp point. For three more verses he takes her "by her lily white hand" down to the bank of some river. This occasionally makes him think about catfish and crappie and all of the other things he will never eat again after he goes to the gallows. He tells her what a wretch she has been for the next 20 minutes (excluding the mandolin solo). Finally, he does what he came to do in the first place, apologizes to his dear old mother for three verses, his minister and scoutmaster for another two, and we are not left in peace until the hangman says, "Now it's Miller time."

Debra drifted off to sleep again just after we crossed the West Virginia state line, so I didn't have to warn her that it is a third-degree misde-meanor to listen to Michael Jackson within a 200-mile radius of Charleston. I simply switched the dial and sang along with the Sweethearts of the Rodeo:

I'm blue to the bone,
Since my baby left me all alone.

Ah, Autumn...You Stink

October 28, 1990

I was going to write a nice, warm column today about autumn.

For several days now I have been jotting on scraps of paper small obser-vations about the season, things like "fire-crowned maples" and "walnuts drying in the fading October sun." I made a few notes about the cardinal lunching in my Japanese cherry tree, and the way the morning chill makes frosty plumes of children's breath as they stand waiting for the school bus.

I was prepared to permit myself to be swept away penning a wonderful rhapsodic anthem to the season -- might have even won a ball point pen set from some arboreal support group -- but then I started thinking about it.

All of those spectacularly colored leaves are now ankle deep in my back yard. Someone has to rake them. Not all of them. Some have piled up on my roof. Those I will have to sweep.

The ones in the roof gutter will soon be turning to a brown sludge remi-niscent of half-chewed Mail Pouch. It will block the downspout and make the "chill rains of October" overflow onto my head while I stand on the patio waiting for the dog to finish her own commerce with nature.

The dog does not finish quickly in autumn. With fall come the squirrels. The squirrels come to eat and hide the "walnuts drying in the fading

October sun." The dog chases the squirrels, yammering like an idiot, tearing across the back yard directly through a swale of stagnant water. The dog spends much of autumn in the bathtub.

Autumn brings zucchini. I hate zucchini. It is fall's horticultural equivalent of the Christmas fruitcake. Everyone gives zucchini. No one ever asks. It cannot easily be stored in the refrigerator because it is usually larger than an NFL linebacker's leg. It is too unwiedly to throw at the dog when she chases squirrels.

Autumn brings the spiders inside. My wife hates spiders. They know this. They wait until she is naked in the shower before re-creating the scene from *Psycho*. She screams for me to bring something to kill it. The only thing handy is a zucchini. I get a lot of batting practice in autumn.

Fall brings solicitors to my door; small ones selling overpriced candy bars to buy new band uniforms. They are possessed of an intuitive knowledge that tells them when people are wet, naked and 300 yards away from the front door. That is when they ring the bell.

Autumn is when we find out what broke during the summer. Furnaces, dehumidifiers, leaf blowers, space heaters, storm windows.

If you think I jest, consider the TV commercials of October. I am mildly annoyed by the one in which a spectacularly attractive woman's antifreeze fails her at 3 a.m. in South Bronx, but the one that drives me to distraction features a battalion of singing furnace repairmen.

They are all handsome, crisply attired, marching down the street of Yourtown, U.S.A., singing the company song. A young and attractive woman (she apparently was able to get her car out of South Bronx) has heard their singing and is peeking out her curtain at the one of them who is better looking than Mark Harmon. They exchange a fleeting glance. She is about to take a sledgehammer to the thermostat. She will tell him her husband is upstairs killing spiders.

Not only do things break in autumn, they break according to Harden's Immutable Law of Home Maintenance. Nothing ever breaks outside the house in August or inside the house in November (the apparent exception to this being furnaces).

I will write no ode to autumn this year. The cardinal perched in the Japanese cherry tree eating its shriveled fruit is sitting directly above the roof of a recently waxed car. Nature will take its inevitable course.

The dog is standing on the back of the couch staring out at the thickening carpet of leaves and the squirrels hiding the last of my walnuts.

My wife is watching a TV commercial. In a few moments she will ask me when we last had the furnace checked.

I hate autumn.

Everett Tate, Progger

October 21, 1988

On the day after Everett Tate hauled his nets down from Manteo Reef to Jack Channel, he brought in 250 pounds of flounder, another 150 of mullet. His broad, earnest face was burned red from the wind whipping across Pamlico Sound, near the North Carolina Outer Banks.

From his perch in his 16-foot skiff, he could see the widgeons and teal, the snow geese settling in for the coming winter at Pea Island. Six more weeks of floundering, he said. Come December, he will turn his efforts to perch.

They call Everett a "progger."

"If you're a progger," explained his wife, Suzanne, "you catch whatever you can."

Everett was a shrimper the first time Suzanne laid eyes on him. He was running a double-rigged trawler out of Charleston Harbor. She was a Navy officer stationed nearby. She wanted to see what shrimping was all about, her own fishing experience limited to her girlhood days in her native Ohio.

"I'll carry you," was all he said when she asked, never expecting her to show up for the boat's 3 a.m. departure.

After her first day of shrimping, she asked Everett if she could go again, explaining she had forgotten her camera the first time out.

They were married at the Navy chapel two months later.

"He was 29," Suzanne teased. "Getting to be an old bachelor."

For eight years they shrimped. Then one winter night, while Everett was bringing his trawler up the intercoastal canal, it struck a log and sank.

Everett scrambled to the safety of the canal bank.

As for the boat, recalled Suzanne, "The Army Corps of Engineers said we had to do something about it or they would blow it up."

Everett's family, most of them Outer Banks fishermen, organized a flotilla of small fishing boats, rounded up as many bilge pumps as they could find and raised the Miss Judy. Not long after, the couple sold the boat.

"Everett wanted to come back to North Carolina and run a bait-and-tackle shop," Suzanne said. "That was always his dream."

They called it Tate's Landing.

"Tate's Landing was non-profit," Suzanne laughed. "Wasn't intended to be, but it was."

The couple lived in the back of the bait store and ran a crab-shedding business on the side, selling the fresh soft-shells to restaurants. But even with that, it was a tough living, and when the postmaster's job at Nags Head became vacant, Everett applied.

The locals said Everett never would be able to stay put at an office job.

Since the first of Everett's ancestors jumped ship off Kitty Hawk and had to be plucked from the surf by a lifesaving crew, the family had always had a taste for salt water, always been fishermen.

The captain of the lifesaving station who pulled Everett's great-grandfather from the surf off the Outer Banks said later he would have thrown him back if he had known he was going to marry his daughter.

Everett's grandfather Dan and great-uncle William helped the Wright Brothers when they brought their first flimsy gliders to Kitty Hawk.

"Dan," Everett remembered, "worked with them, dragging those gliders up and down those hills for about three years."

Everett stayed at the post office long enough to earn a retirement pension, then went back to the water.

Meanwhile, the Outer Banks was changing. Like sea-bound lemmings, vacationers began flocking to its beaches. Developers built condos, hotels, grand beach homes. Some of the locals made a killing.

The Tates, not among them, continued living in their modest converted bait store, even as lavish dwellings began springing up a stone's throw from the end of their boat dock.

What seems to interest Everett Tate is less what man has changed at the Outer Banks than what nature has kept constant: the flounder, the mullet, the spot. Put 100 twirling neon cheeseburgers out on the touristy Croatan Highway, and the snow geese will still come back each autumn to Pea Island.

A quieter time in the life of the Outer Banks has been preserved by Suzanne through several oral histories she has published, along with a few children's books. The books will not make her rich, but even if they did, you could still find Everett heading out for the inlet in his boat at sunrise, working his nets.

The sea birds wheel and cry. The water rocks the skiff. A man could do much worse in life.

A Lot of Bull

September 2, 1990

They buried Calvin M. Ivanhoe Bell hard by the edge of Rt.42 near Plain City last autumn. No casket. No services. They hauled him out to his well-deserved resting place with a tractor and chains. He had lived 15 years and produced 660,543 units of semen, enough to repopulate Columbus with Holsteins.

They say he died of old age.

Might have been exhaustion.

Bell, a prize Holstein bull, rests in the front yard of the production center of Select Sires, the nation's largest marketer of bull sperm. Select's sales for 1989 were in the $20-$22 million range, though no sign a la McDonald's boasts of the "number served."

The production center where Bell gave his all is called a barn, though the facade looks more like a franchise unit for Friendly Ice Cream. I toured it last week with Sue Alderman, a genial and patient woman who is Select Sires' vice president of information.

Inside the production center is an enclosed, environmentally controlled collection parlor.

"We use this as a visitors center," Alderman explained. "You can watch them collect the bulls without interfering."

As she spoke, a pair of Select Sires employees were preparing to collect a Holstein. I was curious about the animal next to the bull.

"That is a jump steer," Alderman advised. "He is a castrated male, and his sole purpose is to be used as the mount for our collection purposes. They allow the bull to mount him twice. After two false mounts you'll see a guy come out with an a.v."

Hmmm. How to phrase this delicately. An a.v. resembles a scimitar sheath, and the initials do not stand for audio-visual. It is a collection receptacle.

A bull is collected five times a week, and each collection is sufficient, after processing and freezing, to impregnate 500 cows. It doesn't take much. A single unit is frozen in a device called a french straw. It resembles a cocktail swizzle stick without the orange slice and parasol.

From storage at Select Sires it is shipped throughout the United States or to one of the 50-60 foreign nations where the company does business.

A tour of Select Sires invariably brings one to the Bull Hall of Fame.

"It is done like the baseball Hall of Fame," explained General Manager Richard Chichester. "We pass ballots around to the staff." The bulls with the greatest number of votes are inducted. Their portraits adorn a hallway wall. Their names draw appreciative nods from those who know the business: Conductor, Big Sky, Duncan, Rotate and Elevation.

"Elevation is the bull that put Select Sires on the map," Chichester noted with a mixture of reverence and awe. "He was the best friend a young manager could have."

Before his death in 1979, Elevation produced 560,00 units. At Elevation's peak, his semen sold for $300 a unit (the average price of a unit is $12). And it is still selling. Elevation is 11 years dead, yet 104 units of his semen have been sold since January. It now sells for $100 a unit, and there is more in the freezer.

Chichester predicted that, by the turn of the century, 95 percent of the milking Holsteins in America will be descendants of Elevation.

"That is his legacy," Chichester said appreciatively.

If a bull exists at Select Sires that is likely to make this nation's cows forget Elevation, it is probably Mandingo. He has passed the 900,000-unit mark and will likely become the first bull in the world to hit 1 million. No doubt, he will be a first-ballot shoo-in for the Hall of Fame.

Before I left Select Sires, I paused out near the entrance to pay my respects at the grave of Elevation. He rests beneath a black marble headstone upon which his likeness has been chiseled. It does not make one feel sad so much as inadequate.

A friend of mine recalled visiting Select Sires and, while studying a portrait of Elevation, being told, "That bull's semen built this place."

At $100 a unit, it might have been cheaper to use mortar.

Of Sex and Stationary Bikes

July 1, 1990

I see by this past Monday's *Dispatch* that Ann Landers is under the bed again.

A woman from Canada wrote the advice columnist a while back happily conceding that she and her spouse had given up sex. That letter, signed "Content in Montreal," threw open bedroom doors from Bangor to Bakersfield, briefly turning Landers' column into a reverse *Penthouse Forum*.

A 33-year-old woman from Portland, Maine, boasted that she and her husband had replaced sex with (I swear) a stationary bicycle.

"Instead of sex," wrote a Dallas man, "we hug, kiss, pat, squeeze, wink and tell jokes."

A Houston woman noted that she and her husband had replaced sex with "Bible study, the Masonic Lodge, Eastern Star and crossword puzzles."

I would say this to you, Houston, Dallas, Portland and "Content in Montreal": If the only time sex enters your mind is when you need a three-letter word for 17 Across, I think you are all about three sandwiches shy of a picnic.

To be sure, there are other things in life than sex. But a stationary bicycle?

I can give you plenty of reasons why sex is better than a stationary bicycle.

1. With sex you don't have to wait until Sears is having a sale.
2. No assembly is required.
3. You can ride a stationary bicycle until the cows come home and still never feel the earth move.
4. It is easier to fall off a stationary bicycle.
5. A stationary bicycle never looks good in anything from Victoria's Secret.

6. Finally, no matter how adept you are, a stationary bicycle will never tell you it likes the way you pedal.

As for sex vs. the Masonic Lodge: Amorous advances can be nipped in the bud for a lot of reasons but not because you don't know the secret handshake. And, though a man may entertain a variety of offbeat requests behind closed doors, he won't be asked to cover his head with something resembling an upside-down Slurpee cup.

I've been trying to think of why sex is better than Eastern Star, but I'm not sure how the women conduct their meetings. Like sex, I suppose every motion requires a second. There, I believe, all similarity ends. Sex doesn't require the taking of minutes, you don't have to sit through a 20-minute treasurer's report before proceeding with new business, and no one will ever ask you to bring a covered dish.

This brings us to sex vs. crossword puzzles. My case is both simple and brief. With sex you don't have to run to the dictionary every 30 seconds. But best of all, you don't have to wait until the next day's newspaper to find out if you got it right.

Now, before any of you go off thinking this columnist is some sort of sex nut, I should tell you that the subject does not consume my every waking thought. Sometimes I think about baseball. I like baseball. I wouldn't give it up for a stationary bicycle, but forced to choose between baseball and sex?

You can't play baseball in the winter. In baseball, if you make an error - however slight - it is noted on a huge scoreboard. Thousands boo. It is right there in the box score the next day.

In intrigues me that in my youth the vernacular of petting was drawn from baseball: first base, second, and so on. But beyond that, the comparisons are few. Pitching baseball and pitching woo are not even remotely similar. Example:

Reds manager Lou Pinella hands pitcher Jack Armstrong a baseball and says, "OK, you're my starter." The key word is starter. Implicit in it is the serious likelihood that if Piniella doesn't think Armstrong is performing well, he not only will walk out and embarrass him in front of 40,000 fans, but he also will replace him with whoever happens to be handy in the bullpen. Moreover, if Armstrong has a few bad outings, Piniella could put him on a bus bound for Billings, Mont.

One final comment, Ms. Landers. Sex may be overrated, but you can tell the couple in Dallas who claim to have replaced it by winking at one another that those are not winks. They are facial tics.

The Case Against Dr. Boyle

June 15, 1990

To some, the only curiosity more intriguing than the Robin Leach fantasy of how the rich live is the engrossing tableau of how they occasionally die.

To that end, on a sticky June day in Mansfield, the curious piled hugger-mugger into the courtroom over which Richland County Common Pleas Judge James D. Henson presided, and watched a pair of prosecutors try to make literal a case for the veracity of the cynical – though figurative – axiom that doctors bury their mistakes.

They came, a few of the spectators, wearing jackets too warm for the season and prejudices too snug for voir dire, spilling out into the hallway on folding chairs borrowed from the downstairs board of elections.

They came to watch the reckoning of the legal ledger in the case of Mansfield physician Dr. John F. Boyle Jr., who has been accused of murdering his wife and secreting her corpse beneath the basement floor of an Erie, Pa., home he presumably intended to share with his lover, Sherri Campbell.

The drama of it all was viewed with a muddle of emotions.

To some, the Boyle case was a real-life soap opera rivaling the networks' afternoon fare.

"His girlfriend is supposed to testify," said spectator and Mansfield resident Betty Palmer, "and there is the possibility of children. I guess all the publicity of her being entombed in the house...I can't remember one case of this nature in my life.

"It was gruesome," she conceded of having earlier viewed a courtroom videotape of the body of Noreen Boyle being exhumed from beneath the basement home her husband had purchased in Erie.

"Once you've been murdered," allowed Dale Secrist, viewing the video monitor of the proceedings from his overflow perch outside the courtroom, "you don't have any rights. They can say anything they want about you."

Secrist said he was a member of a court watchdog group that calls itself Victims in Need of Justice.

He implied that too often justice is compromised by plea bargains traded for convictions. The victim, of course, has no voice in the matter.

"She's not here to defend herself," he said of Noreen Boyle.

Secrist is a friend of Mansfield's Bonnie Rooks, a woman who claims to have attended every Richland County murder trial since the one five years ago in which her son was the victim.

"I had a son killed in this city on Oct. 22, 1985," Rooks recalled with less sadness than outrage. "He was shot seven times, five times in the back...He had just turned 33."

In court, a few rows ahead of Rooks, sat 27-year-old Todd Pittenger, nervously wrapping and unwrapping a brown porkpie hat he held between his knees.

A former patient of Boyle's, he maintained, "I would never figure him to do anything like this. If he killed her here in Ohio, why would he go and bury her in Pennsylvania?

"I just felt there was something not right about it."

Two seats away from him, a trial observer who would identify himself only as "Dave" noted of his acquaintance of Noreen Boyle, "I'm into BMWs, and we became friends, Beemers (the term for BMW owners). We were both Beemers. She had a Beemer, and I had a couple of them.

"Nice lady," he continued, studying the yellow pad on which he took notes during the trial. "Blond hair back in a bun."

"Always with the children," he continued. "I never saw them together. You could tell in her eyes that she was in pain."

He had seen her fleetingly, he said, at Mansfield restaurants and clothing stores. They had spoken.

And so they came, Rooks and Palmer, the note-taking, cryptic "Dave," to see justice done in the case of one Dr. John F. Boyle Jr.

Each had a reason. They knew Noreen. They knew the doctor. To some, it was simply their fascination with a case that embraces all the elements that makes crime tantalizing. There was murder, money, another woman.

They watched the doctor, guarded by a deputy who moonlights as Sneaky the Clown, scribble notes as a procession of witnesses filed past the jackhammer and shovel – exhibits, both of them – resting at the foot of the judge's bench.

In the courtroom stands an easel whose display depicts the clean and precise outline of a house and basement.

To the casual observer it appears no more than an architectural rendering.

The prosecutors believe that, by the time they have finished presenting their case, the jury will clearly see that within that innocuous rectangle a sad and sordid little triangle came to its grim mathematical solution.

The Rules of the Road

April 23, 1990

I was discussing road food with a fellow columnist not along ago when she earnestly offered, "I try to avoid eating at a restaurant where the sign out front advertises shad guts next to the special of the day."

Good advice. Bait stores and greasy spoons do not a happy marriage make.

A columnist covers a goodly share of two-lane blacktop nosing out stories, and the tummy toll it exacts can be exorbitant.

"I never eat in a restaurant that has a sign warning 'microwave in use,'" yet another columnist told me, "Chances are it is the only thing in use."

Over the years I have developed not only a galvanized stomach but also an ironclad set of rules of the road:

1. The simpler the name, the better the food. I enjoyed one of my all-time favorite meals at a hole in the wall in Greenville, Miss., called Doe's Eat Place. If the name is pretentious, they are trying to hide something.
2. Never eat anything you can't pronounce. It is always the first question they ask in the emergency room.
3. Never order the "catch of the day" if you are more than 100 miles from the ocean. A yellow-fin tuna does some hard traveling to make it to Des Moines.
4. If you must eat fast food, avoid the drive-thru. Whatever has gone the longest unsold inside goes out the window to someone who will be five miles away before he discovers the mistake. This is especially true of the coffee.
5. If, upon entering a diner, you spot the cook in a booth working the crossword, leave. There is a reason he has time on his hands.
6. Truckers do not know the best places to eat. Diesel fuel they understand. But food? Blindfolded, nine truck drivers in 10 couldn't tell veal from fried wallpaper.
7. Never eat at a restaurant that has a sideline business. It is not without reason that economic necessity has forced them to take in laundry or add live bait to their bill of fare.
8. Get to know the food chain. Monday's unsold "savory tips of beef" become Tuesday's "old-fashioned beef stew" becomes Wednesday's "beef pot pie" becomes...You get the picture.
9. Unless you want to dine to a chorus of Tupperware madonnas scolding "If you don't eat that grilled cheese I'm gonna knock you into next week," never eat at a restaurant that has more than three station wagons in the parking lot.
10. If the menu features a picture of the restaurant's deceased founder, exit discreetly. It often means they inherited the business, seldom the talent. Only funeral directors should make a living off the dead.
11. Never eat anything smothered in "the chef's special sauce." A lawyer's mistakes go to jail. A doctor buries his. A chef covers his with "special sauce."
12. If a menu item is offered both as an entree and a side dish, it usually is a pretty safe bet.
13. Be suspicious if the waiter's greeting is longer than 10 words. I get nervous when I hear, "Hello, my name is Kevin. I'll be your server. our special is fresh bay scallops in the chef's special tarragon sauce.

It's really quite good. The hanging plants are a nice touch, don't you think? Did I already tell you that I'm majoring in business administration?"

14. Never order coffee in a Chinese restaurant. Chinese cooks never waste anything, including yesterday's coffee. Ditto for iced tea.
15. Don't take it as a bad omen if the waitress asks, "Do you need to see a menu?" If most of clientele return often enough to know the fare by heart, it usually means it is good.
16. Never eat at a restaurant with a window sign boasting "under new management." They haven't yet discovered why the previous owner went bankrupt.
17. Try to avoid buffets. If the chef doesn't want it in the kitchen, you don't want it on your plate.
18. In small restaurants, check the cashier's stand. If the Rolaids box is empty, leave.
19. Never eat at a restaurant whose name doesn't match the cuisine: O'Hoolihan's Pizza, Baglioni's Soul Food, Wandalene's French Cuisine, Nguyen's Kosher Deli.
20. "All-you-can-eat" means "more than we intended to buy." Beware.

Dyschticksia

April 4, 1990

Hi, I'm Mike Harden. I'd like you to meet Ralph and Daphne Koogleman. The Kooglemans, to most casual observers, appear to be a normal, intelligent couple. As a matter of fact, if you saw them at the supermarket, the bowling alley or at home seated around the dining room table working on their collection of poisonous South American beetles, why, you'd think they were just like your next-door neighbors.

Appearances, sadly, are deceiving. For like 50 million other Americans, the Kooglemans are "dyschticksic." They are humor-impaired. Offer them $1 million. Stick a revolver in their ear. They could no more tell a joke than fly.

Some people are able to get by with dyschticksia. They botch perfectly good jokes, but because they are insurance company presidents or Mafia enforcers, their audiences laugh. But average folks like Ralph and Daphne must endure the secret shame and the silence that follow their punch lines.

Fortunately, there are warning signs that help in the early detection of dyschticksia. Listen for a moment to this tape we made of Ralph trying to tell a joke at his family reunion:

"See, there are these two guys and they're playing tennis. They finish the game and they're changing clothes in the locker room when one notices the other is wearing a bra. So he says, 'Hey, Ed. Since when did you start wearing a bra?" And Ed, he says, uh, uh, uh."

It's not pretty. All he had to remember was, "and Ed said, 'Since my wife found it in the glove compartment.'"

The forgotten punch line. A telltale symptom most certainly. Start to tell a funny story to a dyschticksic and he may even concede, "Wait, let me write this down or I'll never remember it." Sad, indeed.

Warning sign No. 2: telegraphing the punch line. For an example, let me give you a very simple joke:

When did the world's longest conversation take place? When a Jehovah's Witness knocked on the door of an Amway distributor. Simple. Right? Wrong. Listen to this tape we made of Daphne:

"This Amway distributor answers his door one day and it's a Jehovah's Witness. They start talking and talking and, wait. Did I tell this wrong or something?"

A simple joke gone tragically awry. Here, let me tell you a nice joke as it should be told:

A pair of duffers are out the links on a Saturday morning. One of them is about to attempt a difficult putt when he looks up and sees a funeral procession going by. He drops his club and puts his hat over his heart. When the hearse is out of sight, his golf partner say, "That was an awfully nice gesture." His buddy answers, "Well, it was the least I could do. We'd been married 28 years."

I tell that joke to introduce you to the most disturbing symptom of dyschticksia: mixed punch lines. Again, listen to a tape of Daphne:

"This Amway distributor answers his door one morning and it's a Jehovah's Witness. And he says, 'Hey, since when did you start wearing a bra?' And the guy answers, 'Well, it was the least I could do. We've been married, uh, no, wait. That's not it. He says, 'That's no bra. That's a duck.' Yeah. That's how it goes. Get it?"

Get it? Dyschticksics always ask because no one ever does.

"Is there hope for these people, Mike?" you ask. Fortunately, yes. Even as I speak, research and treatment go on at the Gerald Ford Clinic, a converted Catskills resort that has helped hundreds of people just like Ralph and Daphne. At the Ford Clinic, dyschticksics start out with knock-knock and moron jokes and through patient and loving care can even make it all the way to Henny Youngman. Show them, Ralph:

"Take my wife, please."

Isn't that great. But we need your help. Millions of Ralphs and Daphnes go untreated year after year. Gradually, people stop inviting them to parties. At work, they are passed over for promotions. They end up in professions where their dyschticksia is unimportant. They become embalmers, actuaries, editorial writers.

But it doesn't have to end up that way. Won't you send a check or

88

money order to this paper today? Make it payable to Mike Harden.
Trust me. I'm a doctor.

O, Romeo, O, Like, Wow

November 8, 1989

My 14-year-old daughter's English class is about to tackle Shakespeare's *Romeo and Juliet.* Having listened to her talk on the phone, I have been trying to imagine, like, you know, how the oral book report on it will go:

This is like a real super sad play about this dude named Romeo and this babe, Juliet. See, they had names like that because it was like real old days, you know, like even before MTV. So, no one had cool names like Heather or Brandon or Shawna. They all had dorky names like Benvolio and Balthasar and Mercutio.

Anyway, these two families, see, the Montagues and Capulets, really hate each other. I mean they can't even walk down the street without thrashing on each other, 'cause, like, that's what happens right at the beginning. This dude, Sampson, who works for Mr. Capulet, he sees this other dude, Abraham, who works for Mr. Montague, and he bites his thumb. I mean, like, not Abraham's thumb, but his own thumb, which in the old days was like saying, "Your mama!" So they start fighting. But it gets broken up before anybody really gets, like, thrashed on too bad, you know.

So then, Juliet's dad decides he's going to have this party. But he has to send this servant out to tell everybody who's invited, 'cause, like, they didn't have phones then. But this servant can't make out the names on the list, so he, like, stops someone to help him read it. Duh! It's Romeo. See, so Romeo looks at the list, and there's all these names of dweebs, jocks, nerds, dorks and motorheads. But then he sees Rosaline's name. She's this babe that he really thinks is awesome, so he decides to crash the party, which is, like, easy, see, 'cause it's a masquerade party.

Meanwhile, Juliet's mom, she's trying to fix Juliet up with this guy named Paris. Is that a dorky name or what? I mean, I thought Dweezil and Moon Unit were weird. But Paris? I guess he's lucky he wasn't born in, like, Fort Wayne or something

Anyway, when Romeo gets to the party, he looks across the room and sees Juliet and like he goes, "Who is that babe?" And she goes, "Who is that hunk?" which is bad, see, 'cause, like Shakespeare already said that they got like "fatal loins," whatever that means, and that they're "star cross'd," which means both of them are Aquarians, I think.

But that don't stop them. So he starts hitting on her, and then they hold hands for a while and, like, he goes, "Oh then, dear saint, let lips do what hands do." And he kisses her, and its, like, super rad for both of them. But then Juliet's nurse pulls her away, 'cause, like, in the old days they got real upset if they caught you sucking face.

But then he has to leave, but he comes back, see, and stands outside her bedroom and goes, "Who left that light on?" or something like that, and she goes, "O, Romeo, Romeo, wherefore art thou Romeo?" And it's like, duh, 'cause he's standing right under her balcony. So he goes, "Do you want to get married?" and she goes, "Yeah." So they do.

But then this dude named Tybalt, who doesn't, like, know what happened starts some stuff with Romeo and gets killed. And then Romeo gets exiled, which is, like, being grounded but like you're grounded in a whole nother state or something.

Anyway, this Paris dude thinks he is going to marry Juliet. Duh! She's already married. But she, like, has to say "goodbye" to Romeo. So she goes, "O, think'st thou we shall ever meet again?" 'cause, like some guys act like they like you a bunch at school but then they never call you up.

Then Romeo leaves and then Juliet is, like, real down. So she takes poison, except it isn't real poison, see, it's like this stuff that just makes you sleep for a while. But everybody thinks she's dead, and, like, they're all bummed out and they put her in this tomb thing.

Anyway, Romeo, who is, you know, like, grounded, dreams that Juliet is dead. He takes off to see her, but he stops, like at a drugstore, for some poison. So he misses this letter that goes, "She isn't dead. She's, like, sleeping."

So he goes to the tomb, and him and Paris start thrashing on each other. And Romeo kills Paris. Then he sees Juliet and he goes, "Ah, dear Juliet, why art thou yet so fair?" 'cause, you know, if she was dead she ought to be green and starting to smell funny. But he takes the poison. Duh! Then you'll never guess this part. She wakes up and sees Romeo and goes, "O happy dagger!" and kills herself.

I mean, are these people serious or, like, what?

None of Your Business

May 28, 1991

My Dear Nephew Mike,

Let your dear old aunt give you and your city friends a bit of advice for the next time someone calls you up taking a survey:

"It's none of your business."

Try that out. It has a real nice ring to it, and it sort of lets busybody strangers know up front where you stand.

Now I know you're asking yourself, "Whatever stirred her up?" I'll tell you. Me and Ott was watching the tube a few days ago when a fellow came on and said – I swear these were his exact words – "In a recent survey, Americans were asked what music they liked to listen to most while making love. They listed, in order of preference, Neil Diamond, Beethoven and Luther Vandross."

You might be able to get away with asking someone that in Columbus or New York or Los Angeles. Don't you people have any sense of shame?

If a stranger was to waltz into the Gas-N-Go and ask a local who he listened to while he made love, why they'd hand him his teeth in a hubcap.

I don't understand you city people. A total stranger calls you on the phone or stops you at the mall and you tell them whether your feet smell or what you read in the john or if you're slipping around on the missus.

Not only do you tell these things to total strangers, you city folks are even willing to pay them $100 an hour to listen. I know. Buster Etlow was seeing one of them psychologists for a while. I said, "Buster, what in the world are you doing throwing good money after bad telling some pointy-headed stranger your deepest, darkest secrets."

Buster said, "Gracie, I'm trying to find myself."

I told him, "Buster, at 340 pounds, you're a little hard to lose."

I asked him what his psychologist said when he told him all these things.

He said mostly the man just said, "Mmmm. Hmmm" or "I see" and then licked his pencil and wrote it all down.

Most people got a few skeletons in their closet, but you city folks hang them in the car window, take them shopping with you. Haven't you ever heard about privacy?

It ain't just that one survey that got me all riled up. Let me tell you what I've learned lately because of you city folks and your big mouths.

About three out of four Americans put the toilet paper in so that it rolls off the top of the roll. Who cares? And who paid the people to ask other people which way they preferred their toilet paper? Is there tax money in it somewhere?

Here's another one. Eight percent of American women do not use deodorant. You people just told them.

I decided to try something just to see if I was off on the wrong track. I called Verniece Mudgett and I said, "Verniece, do you wear deodorant?" And she said, "Gracie, you and I have been friends for about 40 years now, but I don't think that whether I wear deodorant is any of your business at all." I said, "Thank you, Verniece. That was just what I wanted to hear."

I always kind of figured that you really don't have to ask who wears deodorant and who don't. When the air-conditioning breaks down at bingo I can usually tell right off the bat.

Nineteen percent of American men sleep naked. That's another thing you city folks told them. Your uncle Ott happens to sleep in thermal underwear, but if I ever heard him telling that to a stranger, I'd knock him halfway into next week.

Now I know you're probably thinking that I'm a hick and a prude about all of this. That's not the case at all. There are just certain people we country folk prefer to tell, "None of your business." Strangers, mostly.

By the way, just between me and you, I don't like to listen to any kind of music when your uncle Ott and I snuggle. The crickets are just fine. Ott sometimes turns on the farm report, but that's a little distracting, having some radio announcer talking about soybean futures at a time like that.

But that's all just between me and you. It ain't no stranger's business.

My best to your momma.

Love,

Aunt Gracie

You Might As Well Be Dead

March 2, 1990

Imagine, for a moment, an absolute and unrelenting darkness, a sunless gloom that lasts not merely for a day, a week or a month, but for five years. Think of the dreary malaise that besets us all when winter's leaden skies hide the sun for a weekend. Suppose it was gone for five years.

You might just as well be dead.

Imagine a mind sharp and inquisitive deprived of Emerson and Thoreau, unable to savor yesterday's sonnets or today's news. Consider intellectual starvation, a brain robbed of all stimulation save its own inner contemplation. What would you think about?

You might try to recall all of the poems you were ever required to memorize. You might replay passages from Hawthorne or Twain. For a while, you could daydream yourself onto that raft with Huck and Jim, drifting south from Hannibal on the sun-spangled Mississippi on a hot August day. That would work for a week, a month, maybe. But five years?

You might just as well be dead.

How many sensations do you know by touch? The marvel of a baby's hand inside your palm, the stroke of a passing cat, the damp muzzle of the family dog, the soft skin of the one you love asleep in the crook of your arm. Imagine the simplest of them, the ones you take for granted: the sweet, steamy rain of your morning shower; the comfort of an old pair of shoes; the feel of the cool side of the pillow on a humid night.

And what of the tastes? Mmmm. There. A nice cut of prime rib, a sip of expensive scotch, a hot bowl of homemade soup to cut winter's chill.

Think of them gone, all of the touches and tastes you have come to know and savor. You can taste your own sweat, press your face to the wall of your sepulcher. That is all, and not simply for a day. But for more than 1,800 days and nights.

You might just as well be dead.

Have you ever cursed the phone that rings when all you want is quiet? Imagine that quiet is all you have. No music. No symphony. Never the sweet caress of a saxophone upon a favorite refrain. Never the consoling whistle of a train in the distance deep in the night. You could talk to yourself, but after a while even that would start to make you crazy.

Try to envision being robbed of your homeland, being stowed away like a latter-day Philip Nolan of Edward Everett Hale's *The Man Without a Country*. What is the line?

Breathes there a man with soul so dead,
Who never to himself hath said,
"This is my own, my native land."

Forget it. Forget that stuff about purple mountains and waving grain, the flag and the anthem. You have no country.

You might just as well be dead.

Ponder a life in which you awaken each morning to the possibility that you may be shot before the day is out. Put 1,800 of those days together, and somewhere along the way you begin wishing you had the gun, so you could do it for yourself.

Imagine never seeing your family for five years. Your wife was pregnant when last you saw her. The daughter you have never held will soon be starting school. Your father died while you were gone. Your brother battled gallantly against cancer, hoping against hope that he might see you just one more time before it claimed him.

"I don't know how long I can make it," he said in the videotape he made to say goodbye to you. "I don't know how long I can hang on."

Your father is dead. Your brother is dead. You would be a stranger to your own child.

You might just as well be dead.

This month marks the fifth anniversary of the kidnapping of Terry Anderson. He was the chief Middle East correspondent for the Associated Press. His only crime was that he was an American. Some believe he is in the basement of Abdul Azziz military barracks in south Beirut.

He is shackled there among the rats, say those who know the conditions of his captivity. He has not seen the sun for almost 60 months. It has been written that what little he is able to see he sometimes blots out by beating his head against the wall until the blood blinds him.

We have tried to reason with the madmen who did the kidnapping, but for all the good it has done Terry Anderson, he might just as well be dead.

Of Daffodils and Kites

March 23, 1990

Had the windows of the old house on Indianola been opened to the spring of 1920, a passer-by doubtless would have heard the earnest tattoo of the typewriter:

March 2. Still lamb-like. Oh boy! Just wait till the real March winds begin to blow. However, these are the days for kites to be up and out, also for boys' hands to be good and grimy from their marble games. The crop of spring poetry is once more sticking an ugly head from its hiding place.

She was bright and witty, Zora McGlashan; a keen observer of nature; a teacher of history, English and art at Second Avenue School when she began keeping her personal journal of the year 1920.

Sacco and Vanzetti were about to be tried. Thirty would die in a Wall Street bombing blamed upon anarchists. President Wilson had been paralyzed by a stroke, his dreams of America's leadership in the League of Nations thwarted by the Senate's refusal to ratify the treaty ending World War I.

Feb. 22. Washington's birthday, and a beautiful Sunday too. If we could only have some Washingtons and Lincolns to help in the present problems, but perhaps we shall look back in years to come and see that we did have their counterparts moving as prophet's without honor in their own country. Even Washington and Lincoln were bitterly criticized in their own day. Perhaps Wilson will be a diamond of the first water when political blue clay has been washed away and historian lapidaries have exercised their art.

Zora McGlashan's journal, 70 years after she penned it, came to me as a riddle in the hands of local free-lance writer Michael Carroll. It had been passed on to him by a fellow who found it when he was cleaning out a vacant house, The pages, aging buff to brown, were clasped by a rusty paper clip. No name claimed its authorship, but the entry for March 1 yielded a clue:

The boys and girls have the limerick craze. I have been characterized and caricatured several times. They particularly delight in speaking of my being up to date. I don't know whether to attribute this to a nifty blue suit with its tailored vestee or to the fact that fashion rhymes so well with McGlashan.

An old city directory revealed McGlashan's given name. A roster of Columbus teachers of the era confirmed her vocation.

Well-read and a capable wordsmith, she was sophisticated beyond the city in which she lived and worked. Her journal entries mirror the days of a woman to whom thoughts of world travel and a more cosmopolitan lifestyle were a vague, though persistent, dream. Single, and tending the needs of live-in parents whose requests seemed her demand, she confessed the feeling of life passing her by:

May 17. The annual questionnaire came around today as to whether we were planning a leave of absence or resignation for next year. That questionnaire always makes me blue as indigo. I long so much to say that I shall be off on leave for the next two years, but I have almost given up hope that the time will ever come. Thirty years old, gray hairs beginning to come, and brain growing dull.

Almost as though to push such unfulfilled yearnings from her mind, she immersed herself in the pastoral mosaic of a life that seemed cloistered. There were visits from neighbors, church, a new phonograph, the local gas shortage:

March 7. To get our poor frosted bones warm we sat up till 1 a.m. last night. The gas comes on when staid folks turn down their fires and go to bed and when the garages and factories lessen up on their demands. It is a common thing for Columbus housewives to do their ironing and baking in the wee small hours. Even such a thing as a bath has to be worked out at odd and inconvenient times, and sitting up until 2 a.m.

She left a diary of 1920 among the sweepings of a derelict house. She left no survivors to mourn her passing, at age 90, a decade ago.

A few days past, I found the plot and the marker she shares in Union Cemetery with the parents for whom she cared, apparently until their deaths. The stone bearing the name of Zora May McGlashan carries this small inscription in marble: "Spring came and instead of death there was life, peace and joy."

March 27. Went walking with mama out Dodridge Street bridge way. The afternoon was pleasant although extremely windy. I found a stately daffodil blown from a bouquet which was being carried to Union Cemetery. It was rescued from a roadside death to shed its beauty upon our front room from a slender vase beside the ferns.

Sensitive New Age Males

August 23, 1991

The minute I opened the flier for the conference and workshops titled "A Gathering of Men in Ohio," I could feel my daddy's eyes peeking over my shoulder, his breath at the back of my neck.

He has been dead more than a dozen years now, but, clear as day, I heard him quiz, "What you got there, boy?"

I quickly folded the flier and furtively glanced around for something by Hemingway to hide it in.

"Ah, ah, ah. Don't you try keeping nothing from your daddy. Now tell me what this little soiree is about."

"Bunch of guys, dad," I ventured, "all guys, just guys, getting together down near Sugar Grove tomorrow. You know, male bonding. All that shtick."

"Y'all gonna hunt squirrel, play a little five-card stud, tip a few cold puppies?"

"Uh, I don't think so."

"Chase some skirt? Do a little arm-wrestling? What's that thing say? I don't have my glasses."

"Well, Dad," I tried to explain, "this whole thing is sort of about the need for men to get together with men and talk about themselves. There's this book called *Iron John* by Robert Bly and this theory that men don't have to be as macho as they were in the past."

"Y'all gonna wear your colored underwear?"

"I didn't buy that. It was a birthday present."

"Sure, sure. Tell me about these workshops you're talking about."

I opened the flier and said, "This one is called 'Men Moving.' It says 'This workshop asks men to be physically active together in ways not defined by work or sports."

"Well, if it ain't work or sport," my daddy demanded, "what other reason would men have for getting together?"

"How about vulnerability?" I said, reading from the description of the 'Vulnerability' workshop taught by 'movement consultant' Paul Linden: "'We need both safety and intimacy to live and grow. Intimacy is open, soft, and receiving, but that seems vulnerable and unsafe."

"So what does this Paul Linden have you doing," my daddy asked, "if you ain't shooting nothing, chasing skirts or biting off each other's ears?"

"I asked him, Dad," I explained. "He said, 'I might start off by having (the men) throw Kleenex at each other, just to know what they are going to do when they're intruded upon."

"Y'all gonna put a bunch of men together in the woods to throw Kleenex at each other?" he asked, incredulous.

"Not just that," I said. "There is a workshop called 'Men at Play' in which it says 'we're going to focus on cooperation, creative play and fun. No choosing up sides, no put-downs, no losers. All winners.'"

"Who's teaching home economics?"

"Look, Dad," I offered, "men are trying to show that they're not supermen. They're trying to get in touch with their own feelings."

"That kind of sounds like their feelings got sick of their colored underwear and decided to take a vacation to Yellowstone."

"Dad," I protested, reading from a workshop description," 'This technique assists the physiological accessing of the memory centers of the brain. This technique can help unlock old traumas and allow them to be processed, allowing us to replace negative self-imaging with more positive messages.'"

"Y'all ain't gonna shoot no squirrels?"

"I don't think so."

"Can't kill too many of them by throwing Kleenex."

"It's a therapeutic exercise."

"I suppose," he groaned. "They gonna be talking about me?"

"Well," I said, hesitatingly, "there is this one workshop about fathers and sons that explores the traditional dynamics of that seminal bond. It helps us search for a bond between personal autonomy and intimacy.'"

"Does that mean if I was still around, you'd be throwing Kleenex at me?"

"Probably not," I told him.

"I ain't gonna tell your grandpa about this. It would kill him."

"Thanks."

"Just let me know who wins the Alan Alda look-alike contest."

"Sure."

A Good Cup of Coffee

June 7, 1991

This is an anthem to coffee, a hymn to the genus Coffee and its progeny arabica, robusta and liberica. From its trees a bean fruit ripens from pale green to crimson, is plucked and roasted to a raw siena hue, then is ground to an aromatic sand that has jumped-started my waking hours for 30 years.

"One of these days," an acquaintance of mine quipped last week, alluding to the never-ending concern about food additives and dead lab mice, "it will be decided that the most nutritional breakfast is actually a cup of coffee and a cigarette."

Say what you will about it, I cannot think of a single benchmark in my life that did not transpire without a cup of coffee within arm's reach.

I drank it on break while making air conditioners for White Westinghouse. Brewed over an open fire, I sipped it in the woods of Wisconsin as a camp counselor waiting for my youthful charges to fall asleep. On more than one February day at Great Lakes Naval Training Center I can recall wrapping hands around a welcome, warm steaming mug at breakfast.

It kept me awake during the graveyard shift on the cancer ward at Bethesda Naval Hospital. I toasted the fleeting 1968 Christmas truce in Vietnam with a cup of java laced with Jack Daniels.

Like scotch, coffee has a taste that requires an initially tentative courtship with the palate. It is nothing like one's first taste of strawberry preserves or lobster.

Like sex, coffee is an experience that, upon first sampling, may fall woefully short of its much-bandied and long-awaited pleasure.

It took me a while to learn to enjoy coffee without cream or sugar. Now, to add either to my morning cup of brew would seem as senseless as taking a shower in a rain slicker.

No one seems to know when coffee was first cultivated, though some accounts have it first being harvested almost 700 years after the birth of Christ in Arabia, somewhere near the Red Sea.

Americans made coffee so popular that in 1940 it was necessary to establish the International American Coffee Board to ensure that each bean-producing nation would get its fair share of the U.S. market.

It is, to some degree, a measure of the popularity of coffee that with the possible exception of car bumpers and T-shirts, the coffee mug has become the single greatest billboard for our slogans, mottos and personal affiliations.

I have sat at the edge of the sea oats at North Carolina's Outer Banks, sipping coffee at sunset and told myself, "This is precisely what I want to be doing when I die."

In the travels that take me out on the road for my column, I have become quite picky about my brew, judging the various states by the skill of its citizens to make a passable cup of coffee. I have never had a bad cup in Pennsylvania or New York, a good one in Florida or Mississippi.

I never order coffee in a Chinese restaurant. No matter how strapped for time, I never buy coffee at a fast-food drive-thru when I can go inside and insist on a cup from the lower pot on the coffee rack. The oldest coffee always goes to the drive-thru window, there being few consumers who will turn around 10 miles down the interstate to return something that tastes like driveway sealer.

Aware as I am of the fraud and duplicity in TV advertising, I put little stock in the happy claims of the satisfied consumers of Dentu-Grip or Messengill. Yet when I see friends brought together over steaming cups of coffee I find it totally plausible.

I could write more about this, but the last light of June's sun is filtering through my hackberry trees. There is a pleasant lift in the wind, and the dog wants to go out for a walk.

I think I need a cup of coffee.

Goodbye, Arthur

July 5, 1991

Thanks, Arthur.

Thanks for being wise without being arrogant, proud without being vain, gentle though never weak.

I owe you. I owe you for teaching me how to write a breaking story about a fire without being overcome by the smoke of my own words. I learned that to write, "The building was partially destroyed" was akin to penning, "The woman was sort of pregnant."

You, Arthur Bostwick, taught me that unless I was first prepared to use all of all my skills on stories about the letting of sewer bids by the village councils of obscure crossroads hamlets, I would never get a chance to use those skills covering coronations and wars.

You instructed me that because the English language was about to become the toolbox from which I would earn my livelihood, I should treat it with the same respect, care and familiarity a cabinetmaker holds for the implements of his labor.

Among the many journalism professors under whom I studied at Ohio State, you had the first shot at disciplining my florid prose. At that point, to paraphrase Will Rogers, I had never met an adjective I didn't like. I know I kept your blue pencil sharp.

We typed our stories about imagined conflagrations and airline disasters on yellow copy paper, edited them with a pair of scissors long enough to skewer a hog, then reassembled the jigsaw with the brush from a pungent glue pot. The wire service machines clattered like a pair of gag-store dentures.

You never dwelled much on your own journalism achievements. Thus, it was only later that I learned you once explored a Bel Air coal mine with Eleanor Roosevelt, had interviewed Herbert Hoover and Harry Truman, covered political conventions with H.L. Mencken.

In order to get a scoop on a story about the arrest of a suspect in a triple slaying, you once posed as an arrested forger. When a gas explosion in Cleveland killed 131 people, you were the wire reporter who covered it. You once scoured a Wisconsin cornfield looking for a weapon thought to have been pitched there by a murderer. No one thought you would ever find it. You did.

In your fledgling years you were chief, cook and bottle washer for a small Wisconsin paper called the *Berlin Evening Journal*. The newspaper offices and print shop were upstairs from a funeral parlor. When your old flatbed press began hammering out the day's paper, the blam-bam of the monstrosity shook the entire building. Only the downstairs' deceased could sleep though it. The undertaker finally worked out an agreement with you so that his tap on the shared steam pipe would signal you to let the press rest a few moments so the bereaved could hear the eulogy.

It was in Berlin that you first met Leone. You spent 61 years together and reared four children.

By the time you got around to teaching me, I thought you looked awfully frail. You were 69 then, in 1971, a year away from retiring from Ohio State. The frail appearance was deceiving. We had a hard time keeping up with you. When I saw you last autumn on the campus, the frailty was no longer a deception.

"I won't be any trouble when I go," you promised Leone not long ago. True to your word, you died Tuesday with the quiet dignity that had been the hallmark of your 89 years of life.

I remember your disdain for the flowery obituary and how you once held one at arm's length in front of the class and winced, "Golden pinions winged home yesterday..."

They're taking you home to Wisconsin, Arthur.

I'm not going to write anything schmaltzy about it, because that was the sort of stuff your blue pen always scratched out first.

I know it is a little selfish of me, but I wish you had stuck around long enough to teach my son.

Until I learned it from you, I never knew that journalists were supposed to type "30" at the end of a piece so the desk would know it was the end of the story. Sometimes, you suggested, that faithful, old "30" was a better way out than waxing too sentimental.

OK, Arthur.

30

Big Joe

October 11, 1991

This is a eulogy for "Big Joe" Bezilla. Chances are you never met him. Your life would be richer if you had, and, peculiarly, doing so is not out of the question. Big Joe, you see, is still with us.

He phoned from Pittsburgh a few days ago to remind me that during baseball's spring training this year we had pledged to bet a case of Iron City beer on the playoff matchup between the Pirates and the Reds. His Pirates made it. My Reds? There's always next year. He said I'd have to settle for the Braves.

We always bet on the Pirates and Reds or the Steelers and Browns when I was his son-in-law. But I haven't been that for a half-dozen years.

Yet when he was perilously close to dying in the first month of 1990, it drew us together again. Things had healed sufficiently by last spring that, when he lost his beloved Martha, he favored me with the honor of delivering her eulogy.

He sits now in the bedroom of the brick house on Franklin Road in Pittsburgh and looks at her picture, Meals on Wheels on his lap, one tooth left to eat it with, spending his fixed income on a phone call to me to read a valentine Martha sent him in 1956.

His voice is steady when he begins:

A wonderful home, a husband to love,
And happiness all my life through.

These are the things I just dreamt about, dear,
Then we met and you made them come true.

His voice caught at the end, and he apologized for doing what I had to cup the mouthpiece to keep him from knowing that I was doing, too.

Just a silly little verse. Martha sent it the year they paid off their first mortgage. He celebrated by buying her a $35 watch.

Life, I thought, recalling a snatch of lyric from a song, you're so cruel to older people.

I know that even as I write this, Big Joe is in his rocking chair thinking about that great vacation on Lake Erie with Martha when the band played *I'll Close My Eyes*, and they danced until impatient waiters began stacking the chairs onto the tables.

"Look, Mike," he said to me the other day, "if I win, you don't owe me anything. I don't know what you're going to say about me when I'm gone. I won't be around to hear it. But I'll know I owe you."

Nah, Big Joe, you don't owe me squat.

I owe you at least a eulogy, and the problem with us mortals is that we never start to write one until it's too late for the guest of honor to hear.

In a way befitting your nickname, you lived big. You lived with gusto and humor, a song ever perched on the back of your throat.

You had a good glove at second base, held firm when spikes were high and loved the taste of a cold beer when the best man won.

You taught me how to sing *I Cried for You, Linda Rose* and *Darktown Strutter's Ball*.

You tell me, Big Joe, that they've just made a pair of orthopedic shoes for you that cost $350 and that you're not sure whether you'll get your money's worth out of them.

Your days are precious, yet each one is tormented by the ache of being apart in your fourscore years from the woman who heard you snore for a half-century.

I learned from you, Big Joe, not nearly enough, but I learned.

Don't live timidly. Give life not a handshake but a bearhug. Accept the sweat of your labors as tribute for the moments you get to sing *Wild Irish Rose* in the company of dear hearts and gentle people. Love your babies. Marry someone who doesn't mind that you sign her birthday cards in pencil so you can use them again if push comes to shove.

Thanks for the memories, Big Joe. I'm not going to wait until it's too late to tell you I have loved you as a father.

You know, the only thing that bothers me is that you seem to have decided – according to our bet – that whatever it was I wrote probably would have no more worth than the equivalent of a case of Iron City.

The Writing Instructor

November 18, 1991

Sondra Spangler is the last to arrive at the McDowell Senior Citizens Center for the writing course I am teaching on a pair of November Saturdays.

It surprises me that she is there at all, for she is the regular writing coach at the center, and, having ghosted a raft of books, she little needs my counsel on writing.

Yet she attends. It requires no small amount of energy. Only three weeks earlier, she endured her second mastectomy.

"They said there were sprinklings of cancer everywhere," she sighs.

Chemotherapy was started. At 48, she is two decades younger than most of the students she coaches in writing at McDowell. But she is their mentor, the teacher who has steadily coaxed from them the gift of writing. For years, they reared their babies, tended domestic necessities and put any hopes they had of writing on the back burner.

Sondra has been the flame that kindled dreams deferred.

Seeing her sitting among her students, pen poised to take notes from me, I feel presumptuous. But I push on.

We speak of leads, of how important the first paragraph of a personal essay is to drawing the reader into the piece. From my collection of other writers' leads, I read some of my favorite examples.

We talk about writing devices, technique and style. Eventually we reach the point when I ask them to write a lead from scratch. It is short notice, but they need testing.

When they have finished, I ask them to read their leads aloud. Some are good. Some are bad.

"Sondra?" I query. "How about you?"

I know she is sick, know better that she countenances no pity. So I ask.

She begins:

"I won't be seeing you again," he announced, visiting her in the hospital following her mastectomy.

"What?" she murmured through the haze of painkilling drugs.

"You see," he said, "sex for me is a whole body experience and now you're-"

"Get out!" she screamed, interrupting his thought.

She carried that self-image for years until a kinder voice reminded her that she had more femininity in her little finger than most women with two breasts.

I swallow hard, look out among the students for a critique of what they have just heard. A half-dozen of them have turned their faces away. Their teacher, the woman who has been schooling them for years to be honest with their hearts when they took pen in hand, has just revealed how searingly painful the act can be. As well, in a left-handed way, she is telling them she doesn't know how much longer she might be teaching them to write.

A week later, the class meets again for my last session as their pinch-hitting instructor.

I don't expect to see Sondra, aware that she is beginning chemotherapy. Exhausted and nauseated from the treatments, she shows up. Her pallor is not encouraging. She confides she bought a "Jane Fonda" wig to cover the toll of the treatments.

"Hey," she says, "I can still come out on the other side of this."

But the reality that her days may be measured has refocused much of her thinking. She laughs.

"I have a very low tolerance for the B.S. in life. All of the sudden things matter in a different way. I'm not dragging things. I'm saying to people what ought to be said. It is like the layers of an onion are falling off from all sides."

On the second day I fill in for Sondra Spangler, she sits among her fellow students, although the nausea and weariness get the best of her. Every eye turns upon her as she leaves the class to wrestle with the side effects.

This is a class she has taught for years and whose students, but for her love, might never have explored their lives through writing.

"I don't' feel like these people need me anymore," she wearily offers, assessing the progress they have made as writers.

Her energy is a rapidly depleting resource. She wants to say so much, yet all the while aware of the clock.

"Every day counts," she says, "probably every minute."

I cannot help wondering whether I have wasted the time of Sondra's students. For all that I have lectured, I may have helped them little in learning to write. But she, without lecturing at all, has taught them how to live.

Saturday at the Lonesome Dove McDonald's

February 10, 1989

With apologies to Larry McMurtry, I offer, this morning, Saturday At the Lonesome Dove McDonald's:

Capt. Call: (Straightening his paper hat and sniffing at the air) Better git yer gear together, boys. I smell kids on the wind.

Deets: (Bursting through the door) We got company, Cap'n. I spotted 'em just south of the mall and headed this way.

Capt. Call: Comanches?

Deets: Just one, Cap'n. The rest are Dakotas, Cheyenne, Cherokees. All of 'em 4-wheel-drive, carryin' six, maybe eight kids each. I think I saw one Brat.

Gus: (Chewing on a coffee stirrer) Dang your eyes, Deets. They're all brats.

Capt. Call: Pea-Eye, you take the grill. Newt, get the french fryer. Deets, I want you on the drive-through. Jake, I'm short-handed. Yer gonna have to be Ronald.

Jake: (Throwing down his paper hat in disgust) I ain't doin' it, Cap'n. I was Ronald last Saturday and those savages like to killed me. Took a shot from a dart gun right between the eyes. Besides, I can't never remember all the words to *Happy Birthday*.

Capt. Call: If you don't want to do it, Jake, then turn in yer duds and draw yer pay. I got lots of folks here just love to make employee of the month.

As the sulking Jake pulls on the Ronald McDonald costume, two dozen children begin trooping through the door. Customers dive under tables, sneak toward the exit. A nervous man at the counter tries to gather his order in his arms, but it is too much to hold.

Lorena: (Observing his plight) You need a poke, honey?

Gus: Lorie, darlin', it's called a "sack," not a "poke."

Capt. Call: Pea-Eye, I'm gonna need 24 Happy Meals. did you take your Valium today? Newt, you'd better start up that second fryer.

Newt: Yes sir.

Gus: Ease up, Woodrow. You take life too hard. You got to learn to like the little everyday things like a sip of whiskey of an evening, microwave milkshakes, call forwarding. And, dern your danged hide, when you gonna give that boy a name? How would you like to go through life named for a salamander?

As he speaks, the clamor of children is broken by a piercing yelp. A young boy approaches Capt. Call and points to Jake.

Boy: he kicked me.

Capt. Call: Jake, is that true?

Jake: Cap'n, I got a hangover that won't quit. And that little rug rat bit me on the leg. I didn't kick him that hard.

Capt. Call: Ronald ain't never supposed to kick a kid. Ronald is always nice to children. If he starts kickin' kids every time the urge moves him, why they'll all be taking their birthday parties to Burger King. Pea-Eye, Deets, get the rope.

Lorena: Dang! He was supposed ot take me to Zanesville. I ain't never seen Zanesville.

Dish: I could take you.

Lorena: Dish, Jake ain't even dead yet. It don't seem hardly fittin'..."

Dish: I got two bus tickets right here.

Lorena: I'll get my coat.

Jake: (Standing precariously on a trash container stamped "Have a nice day," a rope around his neck) I just want to say that I always tried to be the best Ronald I could. I know I weren't no Fred Rogers or nothing. It ain't easy. Two-hundred-pound man in that hot clown outfit, dancing around like a Dodge City hairdresser. I guess I could say, whoa, look out, arrrrrrrrrrrrrrrrrrrgh!

Capt. Call: Sorry to cut you short, Jake. Lunch rush.

A meek character, hat in hands, approached Capt. Call.

July: Cap'n, my name is July Johnson. Accent on the first syllable. I'm a lookin' for a woman named Ellie.

Deets: I seen her. She came through the drive-through with a half-wit fella. They was drivin' a '71 Catalina, Arkansas tags. Ordered one Quarter Pounder (no onions), one Big Mac, two black coffees and a courtesy cup.

July: I guess she's gone for good.

Gus: Now, son, don't take it so bad. There's a lot of danged things in life worse than losin' a wife to a half-wit: athlete's foot, root canals, summer reruns.

Capt. Call: Might as well stay on, July. I could use a good hand just now. Can you play a clown?

July: Can't be much tougher than playin' the fool.

Gus: I'll thank you to leave the ironies alone. Ain't but one sardonic philosopher in this movie.

July: Sorry.

Capt. Call: Just so you know the lyrics to *Happy Birthday*.

Better Than I Deserved

March 14, 1989

He stands, hands jammed in his peacoat pockets, a beard stubble wreathing a smile just crooked enough to suggest a devilishness he has but rarely let me glimpse. Together we contemplate the old car we have coaxed into the used-car lot to barter for better.

Out on the lot, a sleek, ebony number stands polished and waiting. It quickens his pulse, mocks his savings account. His interest is surpassed only by the prime rate. We talk, and amidst innocuous blather about financing options I am ambushed by the heart-sinking recognition of what this moment presages.

Do you remember, I want to blurt, that sun-washed July afternoon when you saved an extra-inning victory for your Little League team, diving to snare a fading line drive in right field's desolate purgatory? You had spent much of the season exposed to no peril so great as falling backward off the bench you uncomplainingly rode. The chance your sunburned nose had sniffed only as a daydream came swift and unexpected, and when your gloved hand lifted aloft the only proof the umpire needed, I had to turn away.

The car salesman, a solicitous cherub, leads us to a table where mere pen stroke reduces son and father to buyer and co-signer.

It is not supposed to happen this way. Where is the tinseltown tableau designed for such moments? The impatient locomotive, the depot platform upon which awkward feet shuffle and love unmasked reveals itself as a stuttering suitor.

Here, in this cramped cubicle, we disclose not affection, but credit references. The only joint promise we make is to pay by the second of the month.

You were an easy one, Son. In all of 18 years you rebelled but once, stubbornly entering this world seat first, choking on the cord, too fragile to come home with your mother.

In a canvas-and-aluminum papoose board, you slept blissfully through the urgent clatter of a college paper's newsroom while I tapped out firebrand bombast. Now you come to me talking of your own deadlines, page layouts, too soon to figuratively cut your teeth in the same room where you once literally did. I left college full of self-importance, carrying away from the campus far less talent than you will bring to it come autumn. With characteristic modesty you dismiss that assessment, though your prose is the proof of its veracity.

When you turned 12, I fretted and wrung my hands about your imminent journey over adolescence's treacherous waters. Like Daedalus I watched you, callow Icarus, lift wings to Crete's capricious gusts, always with one eye trained on the sun.

There were days you flew alone unaware that the only thing steeling my determination to survive vicissitudes of my own beckoning was the strength I drew from you. I, more so than you, was the one Herakles might have found washing in with the surf.

The salesman dangles the ignition key. Shy and self-conscious, you tender me gratitude grander than the favor.

If this were a Western, I tell myself, I would be reluctantly cinching the girth, offering a leg up that you no loner need. One parting stroke along the withers of your steed, a fumbling grasp for words in a moment where none is sufficient. The boot heel nudges the stallion's flank. You are off.

The fates do not give us children. They're only lent to us.

How strange it seems that the moment I envisioned for years with a mixture of both pride and dread should arrive unannounced in a used-car lot. No heraldic trumpets, none of the epic, wrenching farewells we have been deluded to expect after watching the paper-moon artifice of touching goodbyes in greeting card commercials.

Embrace life. Enjoy it. Shrink from no challenge. Your talent is worth of any and your principles will sustain you through inevitable reverses. It is impossible to hold your faith too tightly or let go of a grudge too soon. Don't dwell too long over either praise or criticism. The latter can teach you if you let it, consume you if you're not careful. As for praise, indulge only enough of it to see its hollowness. In the end, as someone else once observed, no matter how big we get, the size of our funerals will depend pretty much on the weather.

Godspeed. You are a better son than I deserved, a better man than I will be.

The Search for Truth and Knowledge

August 6, 1989.

Dear Diary,

Drove son to Ohio State for orientation today to begin his search for truth and knowledge. Search for truth and knowledge starts with finding parking spot. Park near stadium. Must remind self not to tell son how many students have leaped from atop it after one week of Philosophy 217: Fundamental Concepts of Existentialism.

Truth and knowledge apparently located in Morrill Tower. Knowledge in line marked "A-L," truth in line "M-Z." Decide to get knowledge first. Go through four lines marked "A-L." pay $40 for meal tickets for dorm food. Apparently have gained no knowledge.

Told to go to auditorium. Auditorium locked.

Sit with son and look at river. Wax nostalgic about own college days. Son pretends not to know me. Tell him about riots and tear gas. Tell him many students shut down campus so students would have greater voice in college administration. Do not tell him they ended up settling for a pass/fail in Philosophy 217.

Many people outside auditorium. Door still locked. But each must try it for self then say, "Yep, it's locked all right."

One parent has brought home video camera. Tells son that grandchildren will one day want to see it. Shoots footage of son walking. Shoots footage of son trying auditorium door. Follows son into restroom. Probably only parent in America with home movies of a bris.

Pick up copy of college newspaper. Turn to "Help Wanted" section. Hope son will take hint. Son preoccupied "checking out babes." So much for truth and knowledge.

Strange jobs in "Help Wanted." Alaska cannery is hiring. Big demand for driving instructors and young men for all-male revue. Do not show the last ad to son. May wonder why college is important if women will stick money in his underclothes.

Auditorium opens. Parents separated from children. Man with video camera annoyed. Not son.

Man in business suit approaches microphone and hails crowd, "Good morning!" Crowd response minimal. Man tells them they can do better. They do better. Academia beginning to seem like Amway rally.

Man gives speech on the search for truth and knowledge. Tells students it will be hard. Uses the word "challenge" 38 times, "fun" only once. Says nothing about football tickets.

Lights dim for slide show. Voice-over of students telling why they love OSU. One student boasts of going to library to study every night for three hours. Probably no dates.

Slide program discusses pledging sorority. Shows women at card table playing Go Fish. No beer in sight. Shows women decorating homecoming float. Again, no beer. Shows women admiring citizenship trophy. Producer must have borrowed slides from Bob Jones University.

Slide show ends. Second man comes to microphone. Wally Cox clone. Asks if any students want to change their major. Seems strange question to be asking people who have been on campus 12 minutes, but many line up. Parents fidgety. Children had not told them of plans to switch from pre-law to physical education.

Crowd dismissed. Go to lunch with son at dorm cafeteria. Food servers wear protective gloves. Bad sign.

Eat macaroni and mystery meat. Son eats potato chips. Tough for food service employees to tamper with potato chips.

Tell son he must broaden his horizons, take wide diversity of subjects. Suggest anthropology. Open course catalog to "Anthropology." Find this:

620.08 The Anthropology of Sex. Primate sexual behavior; sex and the origins of society and culture; sexual maturation and enculturation; cross-cultural sexuality; sex in art and folklore; sex research.

Son has come to school to watch apes make love and sororities play Go Fish. Will keep him out of trouble. He does not think this is funny.

I tell him even though I am 42, I still dream of Ohio State. I do not tell him what I dream. Recurring dream of sitting down to take final exam for Philosophy 217 after skipping every single class during quarter. Not a happy dream. Variations include Accelerated Calculus 162 and Insect Morphology 623.

Son tells me he must go. I watch him leave to search for truth and knowledge. I search for bar.

Crusade

September 23, 1993

They pressed into Cooper Stadium carrying Bibles and umbrellas, emblems, respectively, of hope in Christ and uncertainty in the weather forecaster.

They brought fresh-scrubbed children, plastic-wrapped sandwiches and "Praise the Lord" greetings.

Thirty thousand-plus who came to the stadium to see the Rev. Billy Graham filled everything from the box seats to the cheap seats, leaving only a few pockets of empty gray folding chairs in deep center field.

Bursting into a spontaneous rendition of *Amazing Grace* on one of the COTA buses that brought them from Downtown, they came on crutches, in wheelchairs, in strollers.

They flinched at $3.50 sausages and $2 Cokes. If patience was not among the virtues they brought to the stadium, they quickly learned it outside the women's restroom.

A banner-towing plane circled the stadium reminding them that the "Book Doctor" was waiting to repair their Bibles should the service prove too rigorous on the Word of God.

With dusk descending, they warmed to a choir made up of some 5,500 of their church-going neighbors, lending their voices to a reaffirming refrain from *Leaning on the Everlasting Arms.*

As an autumn half-moon played hide-and-seek through threatening clouds, they rose as one to greet Graham, craning to get a good look at the man who last hit Columbus for a crusade the same year the Beatles hit America.

It was a different sort of human wave than the stadium was accustomed to seeing that they demonstrated when Graham called them forward to accept Jesus Christ.

Chaperoned by volunteer counselors, they came home to Billy, from left field and right, from out by the foul poles. A sightless man with babe in arms was led haltingly up the third-base line.

Clutching Bibles and wearing T-shirts that reminded one another "Life Is Short, Pray Hard," they scrunched together to hear the counsel of the man asking them to come "as children" to Christ.

"Oh, God I am a sinner," he asked them all to repeat after him. "I am sorry for my sins. I receive Christ as savior."

When America's evangelist turned from their midst, the Rev. Leo Wagner invoked. "Lord, we pray for thy manservant Billy Graham." Then, with infinitely less fanfare than had heralded its coming, it was over for the night.

A beige cloth was fitted over the pulpit. The stadium lights fell dark, though out beyond the center-field fence a lone light at the base of a flag-pole shone upward on the Stars and Stripes.

The flag snapped now and then in a brisk breeze that waved it toward neighboring Mount Calvary Cemetery and the only permanent population in the vicinity that perhaps has unraveled the sacred mysteries and eternal truths the Billy Graham crowd had come to learn.

Karaoke Madness

August 18, 1993

A service-station owner in the Colorado town of Mead, near Denver, has installed a karaoke machine so patrons can warble their hearts out to the steady tick of the unleaded pump.

I'm not sure which songs might be appropriate to sing while gassing up the Subaru. That concerns me less than the possibility that karaoke might catch on in other places where – because of waiting rooms, holding areas or long lines – we are forced to amuse ourselves while biding our time.

Think about what you might sing if you found yourself stranded for a bit at any of the following:

Dentist's Office: *Beginning To Feel the Pain; I Don't Want To Be Hurt Anymore; Haven't Got Time for the Pain; Yank Me, Crank Me.*

Internal Revenue Service: *Ain't That Enough for You; Conscience; Ask Me No Questions; Break It to Me Gently; Shake You Down; What a Fool Believes; Everybody's Got To Pay Some Dues; Gimme Your Money Please; Suspicious Minds; Nothing To Hide; Taxman; Hand It Over; I Got Stung; There Goes My Everything; Silence Is Golden; Why Me?; Money (That's What I Want).*

Emergency room: *Every Little Bit Hurts; Hurt So Bad; Love Pains; You Be Illin'; Arrow Through Me; Heart Don't Fail Me Now.*

Airport: *500 Miles Away From Home; Expecting To Fly; Eight Miles High; The Letter; Fly Me to the Moon; Destination: Anywhere.*

Sex therapist: *You Can't Hurry Love; You Keep Me Hanging' On; Satisfaction: You Ain't Seen Nothing Yet; You're No Good; We Can Work It Out; Best of My Love; Love Machine; Ring My Bell; I Want To Know What Love Is; Da Ya Think I'm Sexy; Don't Just Stand There; Enjoy Yourself; Even the Bad Times Are Good; Help Me Make It Through the Night; I Don't Know How To Love Him; Whatever Gets You Thru the Night; Sexual Healing; I Can't Do It by Myself; Love Potion No.9.*

Doctor's office: *Doctor My Eyes; Physical; Do You Feel All Right; Do You Really Want To Hurt Me; Doctor's Orders; Found a Cure; Funny Feeling; 98.6; Feel So Bad; Fever;You're My Remedy.*

Confessional: *Am I Forgiven; Confession of a Sinner, Bad to the Bone;*

Theme From "The Exorcist", Evil Ways; Father Knows Best; I Apologize; You Said a Bad Word; Telling Lies; Shame on Me; Sorry; Nobody's Perfect; I Can't Be All Bad; God Knows.

Funeral parlor: And When I Die; And the Grass Won't Pay No Mind; Red Roses for a Blue Lady; Another One Bites the Dust; Ashes to Ashes; Ding Dong! The Witch Is Dead; Knockin' on Heaven's Door; Got a Date With an Angel; Here Comes Heaven; Freddie's Dead.

Restroom: Dancin' Fool; Will Power, I Just Can't Control Myself; For Ladies Only; Where Do I Go; End of the Line.

County jail: Devil Made Me Do It; Counting the Days; Chain Gang; I Shot the Sheriff; Breakout; Busted; Can I Get a Witness?; Does Anybody Know I'm Here?; I Can't Drive 55; Good Morning Judge; Held for Questioning; I Stand Accused; You'll Never Be Free; You Ain't Going Nowhere.

Psychiatrist's office: Just My Imagination; All in My Mind; Crackin Up; Baby Don't Be Looking in My Mind; Crazy Feelin'; Curious Mind; Confusion; Do It to My Mind; Emotional Rescue; Hysteria; Falling to Pieces; Psychotic Reaction; I Talk to the Tree; Mind Games; Mixed Emotions; Goin' Out of My Head.

Divorce court: This Diamond Ring; 50 Ways To Leave Your Lover; Where Did Our Love Go; All Your Goodies Are Gone, Let Me Go Lover; You Give Love a Bad Name; Alone Again; Bad Blood; D-I-V-O-R-C-E; Baby Come and Get It; These Boots Are Made for Walkin'; Na Na Hey Hey Kiss Him Goodbye; What's Love Got To Do With It; Don't Go Away Mad (Just Go Away); Hit the Road Jack; The Payback; You've Lost That Lovin' Feeling; Thrill Is Gone; Love Stinks; May the Bird of Paradise Fly Up Your Nose; Love on the Rocks.

Playing Catch

April 4, 1993

I didn't love baseball much as a child, chiefly because my father did.

I couldn't have been more than 5 when he began hauling me off to watch him play industrial-league ball at this diamond or that around the city.

The gods of the game – who feared, justifiably, that I might commit the unpardonable sin of nodding off while the old man was playing Willie Mays to a Vic Wertz fly – made sure that he often played on the state hospital grounds.

In the pre-Thorazine era of psychiatry, shrinks were as enchanted with the lobotomy as today's 6-year-olds are with Nintendo, and exhibited no sense of professional shame in extending grounds privileges to their success cases if they wanted to take in a baseball game.

Having been rendered incapable of making any more sense of baseball than genetic engineering, these poor souls patrolled foul territory in a night-of-the-living-dead procession, giving 5-year-old boys all the more reason to hate the hallowed great American pastime.

I was not yet 12 when I heaped disgrace upon the family name by getting assigned to right field on my Little League team. Something deep inside told me there was more to life than baseball.

A newspaper route offered me, at 11, the same wonderful and new appreciation for money that puberty would give me for girls a year later.

On top of all that, the chance to see a world beyond Columbus was thrust in my lap when I was informed that if I could sell but 20 new subscriptions to the *Columbus Citizen* I would win an expenses-paid trip to the Norfolk, Va., Navy yards.

My disappointment at falling a few subscriptions short was compounded when I was presented with a baseball mitt as a consolation prize. I felt like a *Jeopardy!* runner-up being sent away with a home game, a "Nice try, kid," and a pat on the rump.

The new glove inspired only more invitations from my father to go out in the alley and throw the old pill around

No mere excuse for male bonding, the game of catch for my generation was a seminal summit conference between fathers and sons.

Fathers, as the late *Dispatch* columnist Tom Fennessy once noted with quiet eloquence in a wonderful piece titled "Be patient with Dad," always throw too hard.

I have concluded that they do this out of the wrongheaded notion that it will toughen their sons for life's inevitable hardships. At 11, I decided that if, instead of being fun, the palm-stinging paternal fastball was nothing but a metaphor for the rude awakenings of adult life, I would show only enough interest in it to placate my father.

Funny thing. When he grew frustrated and gave up on the ugly job of force-feeding me baseball, I started to like – nay, love – the sport.

The incantatory recital of fractures and casts that attended my playing of the game has occupied a column or two before this one. I will not bore constant readers with a rehash.

Age caught up with me, and, eventually, when I went after a fly ball, it was not with the swift certainty of the "Say Hey Kid" but rather – as Donald Hall once observed of Ted Williams in an old-timers' game – "like a lame truck horse startled by a garter snake."

Blissfully content as a spectator, I am occasionally surprised that I have come to cherish what I once so loathed. Opening day can never come soon enough to sate my need for a baseball fix.

When winter forces me to curl up with a good book, I am infinitely more intrigued by Thomas Boswell's appraisal of Walter Johnson than James Boswell's assessment of Samuel Johnson.

I have even learned to savor the games of catch I play in the back yard with 12-year-old Jennifer.

112

I abide by only two rules:
• Always wait for her to ask.
• Never try to see how hard I can throw. She just might do the same.

When His Ship Comes In

May 7, 1993

Clutching his coins, the man who called himself Harry leaned over the curved glass top of the jukebox as might a child perusing the penny-candy selection of a mom-and-pop store.

Punching several choices, he returned to his stool and peered down the empty bar toward a small window looking out on the late-morning traffic on E. Main Street.

Stocky and short, he looked to be 65, perhaps 70. He wore a black fedora too small for his head. Beneath the sweatband of the hat, snowy tufts of hair the texture of steel wool sprouted around his ears. His eyes had the look of amused resignation, as if they had already spotted the water balloon dropped from above and had decided to go along with the joke.

"He comes in here every day," Tommy, the bartender, explained sotto voce. "He drops $6, $8 in the jukebox. Says he's got some kind of inheritance coming."

The Ink Spots crooned *If I Didn't Care.* Harry knew the lyrics by heart and, now and then, whispered a line or two between spaced sips of the blended whiskey and beer chaser in front of him.

His father fought for the White Russians during the Bolshevik Revolution, he said, and fled the country for Canada after Lenin and the communists seized power.

Harry is the last of seven children.

His father, he said, taught him how to fly in an old Vickers biplane, purchased and refurbished to earn the family extra money by taking locals up to see the Ontario landscape for $1 a head.

When World War II broke out, Harry joined the Navy.

He shipped out for the South Pacific, he said, flying Corsairs off the carrier *Yorktown.*

After the war, he heard about a company that was looking for men to do salvage work at the mouth of the Mekong River outside Saigon, South Vietnam.

"They paid your expenses over," Harry recalled, loosing a plume of cigar smoke toward the ceiling. "It was a small salvage company. There was a lot of work. They were looking for gold. They paid you $1,500 to go over and promised $450-$500 a week. I got $280. That was the best week I ever had."

The job involved nothing particularly hazardous.

He met a young woman in Saigon. To hear him talk, a lotus would blush with envy in her midst. From Harry's description, she sounded as if she might have been a working girl. From the songs he played on the juke-box, it sounded as if he might have fallen in love.

"She called me *mon ke*," he said. Maybe, he thought, it was a Vietnamese term of endearment. Then again, maybe, because she also hit him up for money, it was closer to her best pidgin English pronounciation of something along the simian lines.

The jukebox worked its way through *Whispering Grass* and on to another number.

Harry left Vietnam, returned to the States, married and settled into a small-appliance business in Dayton. The work wasn't as romantic as salvage-diving for gold in the South China Sea, but he said the living wasn't bad.

"Could I have one more drink?" he asked the bartender. Another two fingers of Kessler's arrived.

His wife died. He got out of the appliance business and decided to take the savings he had and go to England to try to make it as a singer.

He said he sang in a few small clubs but acknowledged, "I came back to the States with a lot less money than I went over there with."

But he still had his stories about the war and Saigon. And he still remembered all the lyrics: of the Ink Spots, Sinatra, Tony Bennett.

Johnny Mathis was singing *Misty* by the time Harry started talking about his rich and recently deceased uncle from Canada. As soon as the will is settled, Harry said, he will be wealthy — $17 million, maybe $19 million.

He reminded himself aloud to give Merrill Lynch a call to light a fire under his broker. Maybe the guy could find a yacht for him.

The bartender frowned.

Harry didn't miss a beat, talking about expensive boats, listening to *Harbor Lights* and waiting for his ship to come in.

Solitude

August 27, 1993

The dinner dishes had been cleared and a small knot of family and friends was gathered about the table, lingering over coffee and a conversation that seemed driven by no particular wind, when the topic of choosing a mate cropped up.

Predictably, the discussion was forestalled by a bit of impassioned oratory on the matter of whether humans even ought to be about the business of trying to select a mate for life.

"Marriage is an unnatural state," the argument began. "Why would anyone who has lived a relatively pleasant and unencumbered life for 20 or 30 years suddenly decide that they have met someone they cannot live without?"

Atlanta newspaper columnist Lewis Grizzard has been married three times and claims that he has decided that instead of marrying again he will – every 15 years or so – simply find a woman he can't stand and buy her a house.

The motion to abolish marriage died for lack of a second, and talk moved on to the qualities that make for a desirable partner "till death."

Assuming that both parties are physically attracted to each other, what qualities augur well for a lasting relationship?

Honesty topped the lists of most of those assembled around the table.

A good sense of humor picked up more than a couple of votes.

"The ability to handle solitude," I suggested, and I was rewarded with several blank stares.

"Seriously," I continued. "Haven't you ever been in a relationship where it seems that you can't go to the bathroom without your significant other standing outside scratching at the door and whining like a lost spaniel until you re-emerge?"

I exaggerate, of course, but you get the point. I want the person I can't live without to be able to live without me, to be able to be alone.

Too many people move through life taking pleasure or sadness vicariously from the successes or failures of their mates. Their lives would have little definition or dimension but for the presence of their partner.

Ask yourself this question: Presuming that you are married (or living in sin), would you feel comfortable making the following announcement?

"There's a new movie I'd like to see at the theater. I'll see you later."

Two hours, maybe three, apart from each other.

Yet I know of relationships in which no small amount of anxiety – perhaps even a heated little argument – would accompany such an announcement.

Solitude is the natural antidote for the accumulated minor poisons that issue forth over time from any relationship, no matter how successful and vital it may seem.

I am a strong proponent of sabbaticals for married couples.

See Europe, Sail the Caribbean. Study temple ruins in Cambodia. Go live in a cave. Get away. But do it apart from each other.

Six weeks every three years: If you're married, you deserve it.

College professors and practitioners of other professions take sabbaticals.

I've been married, and I've taught college courses.

Marriage is work, even when compared with an analysis of *Finnegans Wake*.

Several days ago, I arrived home from work early to discover something strangely amiss at my house. There was no sign of breaking and entering; no one had painted the walls purple while I was gone. I didn't smell smoke.

I sat down at the dining-room table and thought about it for a second. Then it occurred to me: I was alone. Even the dog was hiding under the bed.

I could run naked, sing Gilbert and Sullivan, eat a half-gallon of choco-late-chip-cookie-dough ice cream and answer to no one.

Instead, I poured a glass of tea and studied the woods beyond my back yard. Nothing moved in the tree line, and only an occasional lift in the wind stirred the leaves.

I was absolutely alone.

I recommend it highly to people who don't think they can stand to be.

Hog Day Afternoon

May 7, 1989

My Dear Nephew Mike,

The dirty deed is done. The desperadoes are in jail, and the long arm of the law in Methane, Ohio, U.S.A. has prevailed. Has kind of a nice ring to it, don't it?

This all started when a couple hooligans from your fair city decided they wanted to rob the Farmers Thrift & Save Bank right in your little old hometown. From what I hear, they had been staking out the place for a few days before they struck, you know, kind of watching the comings and goings from the window seat at the Blue Moon Cafe. When they finally decided they had it all doped out – or they'd had about as much of Marvella Singer's meatloaf as a body ought to have to endure – they made their move.

Marvella said that the two of them were looking pretty nervous when they ate breakfast at the cafe on the morning it all happened, but she did-n't think too much of it until the shorter one reached in his jacket pocket for a tip and out fell a pair of pantyhose.

"I reached down and snatched them up," Marvella said. "I suppose it was sort of strange for a man to be carrying pantyhose in his pocket, but after all they were from Columbus."

She probably would have dropped the matter then and there, but as she was picking them up she noticed that the hose were queen-size, con-troltop nudes with a reinforced heel.

"You know how hard it is to find that color and size at Dillman's Pick & Save?" she asked me later. "I practically got to drive all the way to Columbus every time I want to get a pair. And I needed some for the

Grange square dance on Saturday.

So she stuffed them into her apron and said to the short one, "You just go along now, honey, and I won't let your missus in on the secret that you been carrying pantyhose around in your pocket."

Well, this kind of befuddled both of those characters, but they finally just shrugged and walked out.

So there they are, standing on the sidewalk of Two Pig Run across the street from the bank they were fixing to rob, and they don't have but one pair of pantyhose between them. They must have decided to split them and each take a leg, because when Buster Etlow walked out of the hardware store he said he saw two grown men fighting over a pair of pantyhose. Each one had a leg, but they couldn't rip them apart.

By this time folks were starting to stare.

As Buster was getting in his car, the shorter one climbed into the car parked next to his, started up the motor, left it running and got out. Then, when they couldn't rip the pantyhose apart, each put a leg over his head, they pulled their guns and crossed the street to the bank.

Now you kind of have to imagine this. Here's two desperadoes in the same pair of pantyhose, and even though a queen-size has a lot of give, they still had to move around pretty much like Siamese twins joined at the head.

And that's the way they entered Farmers Thrift & Save.

They stepped right up to the express lane, which was their next big mistake, because Iny Rae Nutter was the teller.

They handed her a note and a paper bag. It said, "This is a holdup. Fill the bag with money and give us all of your blank money orders and traveler's checks."

Iny Rae handed the note back and said, "Can't do it. This is the express line. Single transactions only. I can put the money in the bag *or* give you the money orders and checks, but I can't do both. You'll have to pick and then get in line again."

About that time someone tripped the alarm. Chief Sizemore was just up the street at the town hall when he got word. He ran out to jump in his cruiser when he remembered it was down at your Uncle Ott's for a lube and oil change. They only available village-owned vehicle was being used at the moment to mow the lawn across the street at the park.

I guess you could say he commandered it, because when the bank robbers came out of the bank with a sackful of cash (but no traveler's checks or money orders) he was half a block away and bearing down hard at about 8 miles an hour. They stopped dead in the middle of Two Pig Run when they saw the chief closing in, his gun drawn and pointed right at them.

It took the chief a bit to reach them, there being a governor on the mower engine and all. But he apprehended them, they're in jail, Marvella got a free pair of pantyhose, and if we don't have this kind of excitement

around here for another 10 years it's just fine with me.
My best to your momma.
Love,
Aunt Gracie

A Stone In the Heart

There are murders that trouble the sleep of homicide detectives because of their brutality, their senselessness or their randomness. There are murders whose annoying shadows remind investigators of how cheap life can be on the street.

But the ones that leave a stone in the heart are the murders of children.

Amanda Witt. Six years old. Sexually assaulted. Slain.

Columbus homicide detective Sgt. Glenn Eggleston retires today after 26 years of service. A law-enforcement officer sees a lot during such a period.

Eggleston's investigative career included the strange case of the bandit known as the "skinny burglar," a whippet-thin fellow whose MO was to slide down the roof exhaust ducts of fast-food restaurants and burglarize their safes.

Eggleston worked through the city's banner killing year of 1991, when homicide detectives scarcely had time for a coffee break between murders.

But what he remembers is Amanda Witt. Six years old. Sexually assaulted. Slain

"I've been to several hundred homicides," Eggleston said, shaking his head, "but to be part of the discovery..."

Amanda Witt was the Far East Side girl reported missing in April by her mother. Patricia, after the woman had left the child overnight in the care of 18-year-old David May.

When Patricia Witt returned home late the following day and didn't see Amanda, May told her the child had gone out to play. Apparently satisfied with that explanation, Witt took a nap. When she awakened, Amanda was still missing, along with Witt's car, her purse and May.

"Death has a smell," Eggleston said, wincing. "It is distinct."

Arriving at the Witt apartment to question the mother, Eggleston noticed the smell. The apartment had not yet been searched.

He asked a small group of Witt family acquaintances consoling Patricia to step into another room, so he and other officers could question the mother alone. The friends obliged, moving to a bedroom. While there, one of them opened the closet and found the child's body hidden beneath a pile of clothing.

"She's in the closet," Eggleston recalled hearing someone scream.

"I've seen some senseless stuff over the year," Eggleston said, "but a child's death is really the worst. They can't defend themselves.

"After you've seen the pictures of that beautiful child..." His voice trailed off.

David May, it turned out, had fled the state in Patricia Witt's car. His body was found hanging from a tree the next day in a cemetery near Savage, Md.

"In a way, we were relieved that the man hung himself in Maryland," Eggleston admitted.

"Hey, Short-timer," one of Eggleston's co-workers called to him as they passed in a corridor at police headquarters.

He smiled at the teasing. He's ready to retire. He and his wife will be moving to Honolulu.

He will pack the desk and take down the pictures, mementos and citations from the wall.

"What is that?" Eggleston was asked about a framed medal on the wall behind his desk.

"Silver cross," he replied.

He had spent more than an hour talking about his police career without mentioning that he had been awarded the department's silver cross for bravery after pulling an unconscious woman from a wrecked and burning car seconds before the vehicle exploded.

Sometimes, that is not the sort of thing a police officer thinks about after he is retired.

Sometimes it is the crushing memory of Amanda Witt. Six years old. Sexually assaulted. Slain.

Nicknames

August 16, 1993

I flipped through my high-school yearbook a few days ago and discovered that, of the 59 students who made up my 1964 West Jefferson High School graduating class, only three did not have nicknames.

We had a "Fifi" and a "Kiwi," one "Deano," one "Gino," two "Reds" and a "Purple."

Big on adjectives, we boasted a "Curly," a "Windy," a "Gabby," a "Juicy" and a "Knobby."

On occasion, I dated "Snuff," "Jo-Jo" and "Red" (No.1), whose nicknames suggested that they were coonhounds, not the enchanting women they were.

I longed to date Jo-Jo's friend "Wiener" but was afraid that her boyfriend, "Herby," would hand me my teeth in a hubcap.

Beneath my senior photo in the 1965 Jeffersonian, my nickname is listed as "Mike."

That is a lie. My nickname remains unprintable in either high-school yearbooks or family newspapers.

Too often I heard the name echo down 100 yards of corridor thronged with snickering, thigh-slapping students.

Yet even though my nickname gave me nothing so much as embarrassment, I would not have wanted it any other way.

Nicknames were designations of endearment. To be dubbed "Frenchie," "Slick" or "White Cloud" conferred an unmistakable measure of acceptance, even affection.

Admittedly, the prevalence of nicknames in my high-school years conjured up the potential for numerous hilarious encounters.

I have tried to imagine "Skunk" and "Snuff" penning love poems to each other, earnestly searching for something tender that rhymed with their nicknames.

My older sister (nicknamed "Sarge") had a young man in her graduating class nicknamed "Scabby" for reasons too horrible to ponder. Though it may seem hard to fathom, someone probably snuggled crinoline against his rented tux and Jade East at the "Moon River Prom" and whispered breathlessly, "Scabby, that was wonderful."

Alas, nicknames have gone the way of saddle shoes, poodle skirts and music made to play at 45 rpm.

June will mark the 30th anniversary of the day "Zambi," "Swimmy," "Big Joe," "Cherokee" and "Mr. Sandman" strolled into the gymnasium at West Jefferson in caps and gowns, and sang the Roughrider alma mater one last time.

I did my part to keep the tradition of nicknames alive by hanging one on each of my three offspring. Unfortunately, "Slugger," "Champ" and "Peanut" didn't last much beyond grade school.

My two youngest graduated from high school this summer and could not come up with more than three students who had nicknames among their class of 156.

I find that disheartening in an age in which we take ourselves far too seriously.

I can think of any number of news makers and public personalities I could tolerate infinitely better if they had nicknames. Washington would be much more fun with "Goofy" Helms, "Mush" Thurmond, "Poodles" Rodham Clinton and "Squeaky" Bader Ginsburg. I have already forgiven our chief executive his notorious $200 haircut simply because one might expect such a thing of a "Slick Willie."

Sadly, nicknames – even among my generation – don't stick forever. "Scabby" and "Skunk" are probably happy about that. My life is quieter without anyone yelling my nickname down hallways.

And I suppose my classmate Charlene takes no small comfort in knowing that, when her time comes, her grandchildren and great-grandchildren will not have to hear a minister invoke, "Dearly beloved, it is with great sadness that we have come together to lay Wiener to rest."

Dear Santa

December 20, 1989

I spent the best part of Monday evening poring over letters sent to the North Pole; letters that made it no farther than the Main Post Office on Twin Rivers Drive.

Once a year I gather a stack of hope-filled missives to Santa. I can always count on Corey's solicitousness ("How is Mrs. Clause?"), Jeffrey's confession ("P.S. The chimney is dirty") or Matthew's counsel ("We have a mean dog named Lucy, so be careful when you come down the chimney. Maybe you could bring a dog bone with you so she won't bark or bite you.")

This year, though, my thoughts are more consumed by the 9-year-old in my home who is wrestling with a question as old as Santa himself.

Dear Jennifer,

In the age of my grandfather a girl not unlike you posed a question to the *New York Sun*; a question inspired by the same doubt I now read in your eyes. It was a honest and innocent question that brought an eloquent reply and the now-famous answer, "Yes, Virginia..."

Jennifer, you are not the first to doubt, nor are you alone this year.

Among the letters to Santa I have read this week, there are many penned by children with good reason to disbelieve. One girl asked only for a tree. Another wished for toys, not for herself, but for her little brothers. Yet another requested only food.

"Dear Santa," wrote 10-year-old C.J., "I really don't believe in you, but for sure, I really, really, really need a kidney. You know I'm on a dialysis machine. I'm 10 years old. See what you can do."

Can there be a Santa in a world as cruel to children as this one has been to C.J. and the others?

Your "wiser" friends already have planted the seed of your current disbelief.

I now tell you that they are wrong.

Santa will disappear only when you let go. Yet you have reached a time in your life when he must change for you.

From the year you first drew breath, Santa has made sure that you have never wanted for a bright and bountiful Christmas. Your list was his command. Each year you bravely marched up to the great bearded one and made your requests. And each year you lost yourself in a flurry of ripped gift wrap and tossed bows on Christmas morning.

Now you wonder, "How can one person with one sleigh visit all the houses in the world in one night?"

I won't lie to you anymore. He can't. Not without help.

You see, all of your young life you have had one unwavering concept of Santa. He has always been the bearded, rosy-checked, red-clad character who arrives at the mall on the day after Thanksgiving. That is good, I suppose. It would confuse the very young to have more than one image of Santa.

But you are old enough to know now. Santa is old and young, male and female, black, white and several shades in between. He can be gentile, but the volunteer who dons a red suit every year at a local hospital, so his Christian friends can spend the time with their families, is Jewish. So are all of his elves.

This is a Santa who steps in when the other Santa is too busy. The little girl who wrote to the *New York Sun* learned that. In time she became a teacher in Harlem, the Bronx, New York's Lower East Side. There was no Santa for many of her students, yet not a one of them went home for Christmas vacation without a handsomely wrapped gift from a mysterious pinch hitter for St. Nicholas.

They had all but given up on Santa, yet the little girl who had once herself doubted, helped them believe again.

She even tutored hospitalized children, children with cruel and chronic diseases, children not unlike young C.J.

She could not always save these children from their poverty or their afflictions, but she never stopped trying and never stopped believing that she could brighten it in the way Santa had brightened it for her.

So, who is Santa? The one I'm thinking about now is short, with bright inquisitive eyes, a bit of a tomboy. She'd fit more comfortably in the chimney than the old elf himself."

And the only good advice she needs to get on with her new role is that spoken by C.J.:

"See what you can do."

Love,
Mike

A Plague of Zucchini

September 6, 1992

O Lord, most kind and gracious, I come to you this morning with heartfelt gratitude

For this summer now passing from our midst.
I thank you for sparing my house from the Olentangy's high water.
I thank you that I remained unstung when the bees attacked the riding mower last weekend.
But most of all, Lord, I thank you that throughout this entire summer you have kept me from the plague of zucchini.

This is the first summer I can recall not having received a zucchini from someone. My life is no poorer because of it.

Usually, by this time of year, a half-dozen are stacked on one end of the dining room table.

Gardeners give them to me, apparently aware they won't hear me venture, "That sure is a dandy-looking zucchini you got there, Earl Ray. How much you asking for it?"

Zucchini is an impractical vegetable. If God wanted us to eat zucchini, why did he make them too big for the vegetable bin?

The zucchini I get remind me of outfielder Kirby Puckett's arm – if Puckett's arm were green (it isn't) and of no redeeming value (ditto).

At least two villages in Ohio have annual festivals to honor the zucchini. Entire weekends are given to the preparation and sale of zucchini bread, zucchini burgers and zucchini ice cream. They likely crown a zucchini queen, who cries earnest tears as the tiara is placed on her head and she is presented with a dozen long-stemmed zucchini for her walk down the the runway.

It might be comical to watch, but I try to keep at least 20 miles between me and any affair selling zucchini on a stick.

Strange thing about zucchini: Those who foist it upon unsuspecting friends do so with an air of immense beneficence far exceeding the gift's worth.

They become animated and vivid – nigh to breaking down altogether – when they describe how they protected from insects a squash that no self-respecting bug would touch.

This, of course, makes it difficult to refuse their gift: "Zucchini? Thanks, really, but I've already got one. We're using it as a doorstop."

Such insolence in the face of a zucchini grower merely invites a vigorous recital of the dishes that can be prepared to showcase his favorite squash.

Not unpredictably, the recipes for those dishes include vast amounts of spices, sauces and cheeses. For tasting a zucchini unadorned is akin to savoring the sweet essence of the small plastic nuggets that shippers use to insulate fragile cargo from the shock of rough handling.

Restaurant owners seem to know that zucchini is a cheap date as a side dish because the vegetable begins appearing with "today's special" in July and rarely goes away before the holidays.

As a precaution, I have lately taken to driving to and from work with the car windows up and the sunroof closed. No telling when some zucchini gardener, in a random drive-by incident, might try to fling something into my car.

Not long ago, I read that, although Christopher Columbus began his first voyage to the Americas with three ships, he returned to Spain with only two.

Put two and two together.

He arrived in the Bahamas at harvest time. He suspected the inhabitants too simple to realize they were about to become an occupied territory. He had promised Queen Isabella he would return with great treasures in exchange for her pawning her jewels to finance his voyage. He had to take back something.

I'm certain the Bahamians were only too happy to load the *Santa Maria* to its gunwales with garden leftovers. Under such weight, it sank in December 1492.

I have heard little about treasure hunters trying to retrieve the cargo.

Growing Up Poor

January 27, 1992

Every time I hear an embittered old geezer lament, "I don't know what's wrong with today's young people," I want to respond, "They have never worn hand-me-downs, never tasted beans, never fixed a flopping shoe sole with duct tape. In short, they have never known the soul-tempering experience of poverty."

Of course, the poor are among us and always will be. I'm talking about the children of the middle class.

I got to thinking about this while watching yet another gloomy economist predict that belt-tightening days are ahead for the average family.

I would never wish economic hardship upon anyone, and I empathize with the plight of those who suffer its sting. But I would be lying if I said I didn't believe that sacrifice and deprivation can teach the young.

The Ohio State University students to whom I teach a humor-writing course one weekend each summer always look at me with perplexity when I tell them that poverty is a good writing coach and, quite likely, the best teacher of humor writing.

If I had never been poor, I probably would have become a securities lawyer.

Trudging off to elementary school wearing hand-me-down blouses, I quickly learned to play the clown. You exchange far fewer split lips and broken teeth if they are laughing with you instead of at you.

Hardship teaches sharing. You need a bat, ball and glove to play baseball, but I cannot recall a kid in my West Side neck of the woods who owned all three. So we shared. If we had had money and Nintendo in our day, we would have learned far less about the give and take of relationships.

Poverty made us inventive. A tree limb could be a gun, a sword, a fishing rod.

Hard times taught us to pull together. Adolescents learn quickly that they are not the center of the universe when necessity teaches them that they have a part in keeping the family afloat.

I loathed toting my mother's crochet work on my newspaper route, trying to sell it to customers. But I knew that the money it raised helped put food on the table.

I sold greeting cards, religious plaques, flower seeds. After the sixth grade I never asked my parents for money for clothing and never thought my life pitiable because of it.

I recall a Christmas when I raked in a whopping $42 in tips from my newspaper customers. Such a sum was unfathomable. I spread it on the bunk bed and just looked at it for an hour.

I thought about the Christmas windfall a few years ago, when my daughter asked whether she could have a girlfriend spend the night. After we had picked up her friend, the two asked whether I would stop at a convenience store so they could buy candy. Her 11-year-old friend, it seems, had just been given her allowance.

They were not long in the store before her friend stalked out, complaining about the place's change-making policy and asking whether *I* could break a $50 bill.

The great irony of growing up poor is that we often waste some of its most important lessons when we become parents. Recalling the sting and shame of hardship, we vow that it is something our children will never have to face. Our desire is to be protective. In fact, we become indulgent.

Also, if we grew up hearing when-I-was-your-age sermons about deprivation during the Depression, we sometimes tend to avoid reminding our children of the tough times we endured. We would rather be cool and slip them the $20 bill or lend them the credit card than seem to be a yammering old harpy, totally out of touch with today's youth.

Well, the economist may be right. There may be belt-tightening days ahead. I don't envy the worry that that will create for heads of households. But it may just teach their children a few things that only hardship can.

"Harvesting" Deer Hunters

October 2, 1989

After a group of animal rights activists in Maryland were arrested for confronting bowhunters on public land, *New York Daily News* columnist Roger Simon is reported to have observed, "You can...shoot an arrow into a deer's eyeball. That's legal. It is *illegal* to speak the words: 'I don't think you should shoot that arrow into a deer's eyeball'"

Hmmm.

I must confess, as a concerned citizen of Ohio, that it troubles me to witness the dramatic increase in the number of deer hunters over the past few years. To use the rationale they have traditionally espoused, I think it might not be a bad idea to find a way to thin the deer hunter population, to help stave off their inevitable starvation by – what is their word for it – "harvesting" them.

Their own annual efforts at harvesting each other is commendable (I refuse to drive my beige Honda on country roads on opening day), but something more is needed. I propose that the Ohio Department of Natural Resources adopt a set of regulations and issue licenses that would permit animal rights activists to harvest deer hunters.

The regulations would monitor and control the use of deer hunter entrapment techniques such as the "beer blind." The beer blind is simply a flimsy plywood structure designed to resemble a beverage drive-through. Animal rights activists, hiding in the bushes near the blind, simply waiting for the honk of a 4x4 and pick off their prey.

Guidelines would have to be established on the use of decoys. I can envision both male and female decoys. The male decoy might be nothing more than a castoff department store mannequin garbed in L.L. Bean factory seconds. More sophisticated versions would feature a built-in cassette recorder that plays small talk about the Browns running game, interspersed with rude body noises and occasional interjections of "Whoa, Earl. Easy, on that stuff. Save a swallow for me."

The female decoy would be one of those inflatable dates sold by adult bookstores. A deluxe version might also feature a built-in cassette recording to lure the prey: "Hey, honey, is that a gun or..." You get the picture.

Here are the rest of my rules:

1. The legal limit for an activist holding a valid Ohio license to harvest deer hunters shall be one per season.

2. Winging or creasing a prey, or inadvertently shooting someone weeding his marijuana plants, shall not count against an activist's legal limit.

3. During primitive weapons season, hunters may be taken using only the following: bow and arrow, catapult, mace, thumbscrew or dropped bowling ball.

4. Hunters who bag their limit during primitive weapons season shall not be permitted to hunt later during deer gun season (or later during low-yield nuclear warhead season). However, should a primitive-weapons activist merely wound his prey (say, the bowling ball only stuns the hunter), the activist shall be permitted to return during deer gun season and finish the harvest.

5. To give the prey a sporting chance, it shall be illegal to shoot at a hunter while he is incapacitated (changing a flat tire, relieving himself against a tree).

6. Once bagged, the hunter must be strapped to the left front fender of the activist's vehicle, wrists tied to the front bumper, ankles to the rearview mirror. The prey must then be taken to the nearest Ohio Department of Natural Resources tagging station. There, ODNR workers will remove wallet, ID and NRA membership card to help them better monitor the general composition, foraging and mating habits of the hunter population in Ohio.

7. During open season, it shall not be permissible to stalk hunters shouting, "Happy hour. I'm buying." ODNR believes not only that such a ruse places the activist at an unfair advantage, but also that it would cause numerous hunters to harvest themselves while crashing through the underbrush trying to reach the sound of the voice.

8. Finally, all hunters shall be required to wear bright plaid or Day-Glo attire. For that reason, it is suggested that portly used car salesmen and rural state legislators stay inside for the duration of the season.

Growing Old

June 23, 1989

Slouched in the barber chair, half asleep, I listen to the familiar thrum of the electric clippers. Harry, my barber, studies my face with the mild pleasure of a physician who has just performed the world's first successful surgical reattachment of a head. I drop my gaze to the shavings on the shampoo cape tied at my neck, and am stunned.

"Gray," I complain. "My beard is turning gray."

Harry seems unconcerned that I am getting old.

I study my face in the mirror. I could shave off the graying beard, but it is camouflage for the dewlap under my chin. There are sandbags under my eyes, and gravity is getting the best of my middle.

I'm getting old, I tell myself. All the fabled symptoms I have read about are there. When the phone rings on Saturday night, I hope it's *not* for me. When I dim the lights it is, more often than not, to save electricity. Occasionally I will hear a song to which I know the lyrics, but I can never sing it because the dentist's hands are in my mouth.

"You're not getting old." Debra assures me, but her gaze is fixed on the spot where forelock is steadily giving way to more and more forehead.

Standing in line at a fast-food restaurant, I discovered a Golden Buckeye card on the floor. Before I could explain to the clerk I was merely returning it, he tried to give me a 10 percent discount.

Beautiful young women approach me and ask, "Are you Mike Harden?"

"Yes," I smile, sucking in my stomach.

"Can I get your autograph?" they ask.

I sign my name and am wondering if I should add my phone number when they explain, "It's for Grandma. She reads everything you write."

It isn't so bad, I console myself. Everyone I grew up with is getting old. Bob Dylan just turned 48. Had Elvis lived, he would be a grandfather. Chuck Berry is eligible for Social Security.

We're all getting there.

They day will come when Dolly Parton enters a crowded room and people look first at her shoes.

Women will pass Jim Palmer on the street and try not to imagine how he looks wearing nothing but Jockey shorts.

Someday I will climb aboard an elevator and hear a Muzak rendition of MoJo Nixon's *Debbie Gibson Is Pregnant With My Two-Headed Love Child*.

And Debbie Gibson will be endorsing liver-spot remover.

Pam Dawber will look at Mark Harmon's paunch and say, "Honey, do you really think you ought to be wearing that Speedo."

Sean Penn will be clubbing paparazzi with a rolled copy of *Modern Maturity*.

Bo Derek will be a "3."

Skin heads will be buying Grecian Formula.

Jon Bon Jovi will refuse to perform unless his dressing room is stocked with Metamucil.

Rob Lowe won't be able to give away his homemade videotapes.

Arnold Schwarzenegger will have trouble with jar lids.

Madonna's beauty mark will be just another wart.

Mick Jaggar will be wearing adult diapers.

Ricky Shroder will be worried about gum disease.

Michael Jackson won't have any hair to burn.

Grace Jones will be shocked at the way young people dress.

Cyndi Lauper will be thinking about pre-need burial plans.

Bruce Springsteen will be doing American Express commercials.

Daryl Hannah will be the official spokesman for the American Association of Retired Persons.

All of the supermarket tabloids will be speculating about the decision by Chuck and Di to live in separate nursing homes.

Jane Fonda will have cellulite.

The Fat Boys will be fat old men.

John McEnroe still will be unpleasant.

Eddie Murphy will hide videotapes of his concerts from his grandchildren.

Mikhail Baryshnikov will miss with the flyswatter.

At the beach, people will kick sand on Mike Tyson.

The little, old gray-haired lady Don Johnson helps across the street will be his wife.

What makes Clint Eastwood's day will be All Bran.

Harry "The Accident" Gordon

March 1, 1991

I wanted to interview Harry "The Accident" Gordon. I just didn't want to do it around combustible material, in moving traffic or during an electrical storm.

"Everybody says he's got nine lives," said his wife, Fran, her voice colored with awe as she glanced admiringly across the living room at her 88-year-old husband. Harry smiled in acknowledgement, crinkling once-singed eyebrows around a scar the size of a quarter. Seated in an easy chair with no sharp edges, he seemed safe for the moment.

It was 1921 when "The Accident" found his first good place to happen.

"I was working for the S.S. Kresge Co.," Gordon recalled from his Clintonville home. He had stowed a load of boxes on the freight elevator of the Downtown Columbus department store, hopped aboard and pulled the chain to lower the protective gate. It came down squarely on his foot.

"My shoe went down the elevator shaft," he explained. "I couldn't see my foot, because it was between the elevator and the shaft." The conveyance jerked haltingly upward, mangling Harry as it went. He limped off at the first stop: kitchenware, sheet music and women's foundation garments.

The sheet music clerk, seated at her piano bench, took one look at Harry, grabbed the microphone through which she had been warbling *Alexander's Ragtime Band* (or some such ditty) and in rising contralto asked if there was a doctor in the store.

"The foot will have to come off," Gordon said he was told on arrival at Grant Hospital. But when he emerged from the anesthetic, he discovered it had somehow been saved.

When he left Grant, after an extensive stay, he was told he would have a limp throughout his life.

Two years later, he was not only walking without a limp but also running. As a matter of fact, he remembers that he was running when he bounded into the woods during a hayride at Hayden Falls and stepped off the edge of a cliff. He fell the equivalent of three stories. A scraggly tree growing out from the shale face of the cliff broke his fall and his arm. He was unconscious when they found him.

On the Fourth of July, in 1929, he was tamping shot into the muzzle of a homemade cannon he had fashioned from a length of automobile axle, when it went off. The blast, which all but amputated an index finger, left him singed, seared, stunned and standing in the smoke like a bad impersonation of Wile E. Coyote.

Two decades later, he was managing a service station on Lane Avenue, when it blew up. A natural gas leak had seeped into the porous soil beneath the station and spread throughout the cinderblock honeycombs of the structure. Gordon had closed the station no more than five minutes before the blast to go fetch an order at an auto parts store.

The concussion left nothing standing save a ragged, shoulder-high stretch of cinder blocks that once had been the back wall. Spark plugs, fan belts and wrenches came to earth more than 100 yards away at what is now the mid-court stripe of St. John Arena.

He stood disbelieving among the throng of gawkers, as firemen, using long-handled rakes, sifted the rubble for human remains. Someone among the crowd recognized him and hollered, "There he is now!"

"And, of course, then the firemen stopped raking," he said.

Then there was the night back in 1955 when, returning from a fishing outing, he was broadsided on Olentangy River Road. Thrown from his car, he skidded along 60 feet of asphalt and gravel, coming to rest a stone's throw from the front door of what was then WLWC-TV studios. He remembers that a youthful, eager TV reporter named Jimmy Crum presided over the preservation of that calamity on news film.

Not long after that, during a middle-of-the-night trip to the bathroom, he took a wrong turn and stepped sleepily off the second-floor landing.

He was helping push a car out of the snow during the winter of 1968 when a board placed under a rear wheel for traction rocketed out from the spinning tire and shattered his ankle.

A week after Thanksgiving last year, his Plymouth was totaled on Indianola Avenue when hit from behind. His back still bothers him from that.

During my chat with Gordon, I presumed that the scars dotting his face were from accidents. No, he corrected me; his long years of working outdoors had caused several growths of skin cancer. Implying it was more a nuisance than a threat, he began counting the scars.

"One, two, three," he started, marking each site with the index finger he had almost lost to the cannon. "Four, five, six, seven. Why don't we just call it five?"

I decided I could see myself to the door without his help.

Super Lotto

November 10, 1991

Whew! That was close. I almost won $24 million in the Super Lotto last night. I played my Social Security number, my family's ages. I divided my blood pressure by my underwear size. And, if only five numbers had been different, I would be rolling in greenbacks, up to my eyes in moolah. I'd be lighting my cigars with dead presidents. In short, I'd be miserable.

I should explain.

For years, I have been trying to win. The Super Lotto was going to be my ticket to a home on the Carolina Outer Banks, a trip to Paris, the Lamborghini. Each time I saw a price tag beyond my means I would sigh, "Well maybe I'll hit the Lotto."

But what if I did?

Oh, at first there would be a champagne fight with a lot of whooping and shouting and high-fives all around. The newspaper would take my picture presenting the winning ticket to a lottery official above the caption "Retired columnist."

I would pay off the bill with the first year's check ($706,153 after taxes), but there would still be wads of cash left over, a fact not to be lost on third cousins I haven't seen since the Carter administration. They would show up, wanting me to invest in one of those pyramid deals in which you sell home-cleaning products so safe that the tub-and-tile foam can be served as meringue.

My oldest son would decide that two years at The Ohio State University is enough, and, instead of pursuing his journalism degree, he would borrow enough money to open a Short North gallery where impressionable securities lawyers pay an arm and a leg for abstract elk dung paperweights.

The younger children would decide not to even bother with college. They would fall in with a coterie of gentrified adolescents who have big cars, small pupils and far too much time on their hands.

The mailbox would be routinely jammed with invitations to parties where people eat fish eggs, drink designer water and pout about the difficulty in finding reliable domestics. The bartender at these soirees would be some kid in a tuxedo who has just read for the lead in a musical adaptation of *Elephant Man* and is bartending only until he can find a role that will truly showcase his dramatic gifts.

No matter how much money I donated to charity, I would still be hounded by rain-forest activists and whale people.

Congressmen would telephone and chat as though we were old Army buddies. They would ask me to fund-raisers at which it would be hinted that a generous campaign contribution could open the door to an appointment as protocol attache to the U.S. Embassy in Bangkok.

As a result of attending this fund-raiser, my picture would appear in *Vanity Fair* and later be seen by Snake and Digger a week before their parole. They would be nice enough to put a blanket in the trunk so I wouldn't catch cold while they're negotiating the ransom.

Their first attempts to reach Debra and make their money demands would be unsuccessful, because the home phone would be tied up by someone from the Save the Snow Leopard Foundation making their own money demands.

Once a drop site for the ransom had been established, the kidnappers would leave me to stumble about the woods, hands tied, a blanket over my head on the first day of deer season.

After surgeons removed the slug from my backside, I would be sent home to recuperate.

Propped on my pillows, bored to tears, I would flip open the latest *Vanity Fair*, spot Debra's photograph and read: "Former bartender Keith Ashton escorted Debra Harden to Pia Zadora's rain-forest fund-raiser. Harden's husband is recuperating from a wound suffered in a freak hunting accident. Ashton will star in the off-Broadway production of *Pachyderm Nights!*, a musical funded by the Debra Harden Foundation for Showcasing the Dramatic Gifts of Young Male Talent."

The worst thing about this rude awakening is that I wouldn't even have a column in which to describe my misery.

It all might have happened if I hadn't been lucky enough to lose last night's Lotto.

The Con's Tale

January 1, 1991

"They popped Joey Naples," he said, borrowing one of my Marlboros and neatly slicing off the filter with his pocketknife. "'Doc'" Sam Sheppard died, Yonnie Licavoli died. I don't know about 'Wop' English, 'Boo-hoo' Dempsey."

He cradled his coffee cup as gently as one might a fallen bird, yet with a paw large enough to easily suggest why he was once call "Bull."

We talked at a McDonald's near the county line because the subject of his reminiscences has occasioned his wife enough grief over the long years of their marriage. She is deeply involved with the church. At 72, he hasn't pulled a job in years, but sometimes he gets to thinking about the times he had and the time he did for it.

He pulled two stretches in Ohio, one in Kentucky and one in the federal correctional facility in Atlanta.

When the controversy arose recently about whether to allow public tours of the abandoned Ohio Penitentiary, his sentiments were never in doubt.

"I kind of wanted to go over to that old place," he admitted. "I wanted to see if the little Catholic chapel is still there, and James Hospital."

When he came out of prison for the last time in the mid-60's, he let go of it all.

"You know what will get you?" he asked with a half-smile. "You get religion or you start thinking about your poor old mother or your wife. I wasn't a bad husband. I loved my wife and children. All she asked was for someone to pull with her in the harness.

"I just loved that fast buck," he said.

That was what landed him and "Frisco" in the Kentucky correctional facility at LaGrange in '42. They were, he wistfully recalled, among the last Kentucky prisoners to actually wear stripes. But when the wardrobe grew tedious, they commandeered a bread delivery truck and tried to crash it through the prison gates.

"Bull" was at the wheel, with "Frisco" and "Slim" piled into the front seat beside him. "Dunk," the youngest, crouched on the floorboards where it was thought he'd be least likely to be hurt.

"Bull" rammed the gate three times. It wouldn't give. The guards opened up with a fusillade. "Slim" was hit in both legs. "Frisco" took a bullet. "Dunk" went out with a bullet that slammed through his rib cage and into his heart.

"Bull" rolled up his sleeve and pointed out a nickel-sized scar on his left arm just above a tattoo of praying hands. The other shot hit him in the backside.

Transferred to a more secure facility near Eddyville, Ky., he and "Frisco" tried again, wiring castoff spring mattresses end to end and, during a driving rainstorm, flinging them against the high fence like a scaling ladder. He still carries in his leg a souvenir from the gun of the guard who stopped him before he made it over the top.

After parole in Kentucky, he moved his act to Ohio, where he and a bunch of his running mates known as the "Irish Mafia" tried to prove that no safe in Columbus actually was.

He preferred stealth to confrontation, picks and jimmy bars to guns. But it all caught up with him.

"We got to the point," he complained, "where we couldn't even carry our tools in the car because that was a one-to-seven (years)."

In 1963, during a stint in the Ohio Pen, he was out in the yard when he witnessed the guards escorting to a death house holding cell the last man executed in Ohio's electric chair.

"I saw poor Donald Reinbolt," he remembered, "on his last walk. They were taking him from the blocks to the death house. He was just looking up at the birds and the sky." It was as though he was trying to catch one final glimpse of the world.

That is past now. Donald is long gone and Frisco settled down. Among absent friends, he recalled that "Lloyd is also dead" and "Casey fell and broke a hip."

"We was just a bunch of thieves," he confessed. "That's all there is to it."

But he is a church man now, and the wife doesn't care for talk about his past. Still, he mused nostalgically, "I've been in some of the finest homes in Columbus."

Cat Bashing

February 22, 1991

I have been accused of cat bashing.

Don't misunderstand. It is not as though the Humane Society has hidden camera footage of me going after an Abyssinian with a Weed Easter.

No, one of my readers, in a terse little note about the size of a fur ball accused me of a mean-spirited bias against felines. I had made mild sport of a domestic cat mishap, and she (I never get pro-cat letters from men) intimated that she had been keeping an eye on the column and had documented other incidents of cat bashing. I suppose the Right To Purr lobby now has a thick dossier on me.

I do not dislike cats. I confessed as much last week at a social gathering to a woman who has seven of them. Her cats – I swear this is true – were part of her prenuptial agreement. I imagine she got to worrying about what might befall them in the event of her untimely demise, maybe started thinking about her new husband sneaking out to the cesspool at night with all seven cats and her Lady Ebonite cinched inside a feed sack, and decided to put things in writing.

I would never harm a cat. Can we get that on the record? As to why I prefer the company of dogs, most of it boils down to one basic fact: Cats won't fetch.

Try it. Take your Siamese out in the back yard, show it a stick and then throw it (the stick).

The cat will appraise you with the bored impatience of Marlon Brando listening – as his fettuccine grows colder by the moment – to a double-crossing Mafia underling begging for his life.

Dogs will fetch. My dog will fetch anything I throw: tennis balls, rubber bones, dirty socks. She would go after a hand grenade if I threw it.

Cat owners have just read the previous sentence and are now stroking Pooter behind the ears explaining, "See, love drop. Mr. Harden likes dogs because they are so dumb."

Well, yeah. It's true. Of course, Pooter's owner would have us believe that in the privacy of the litter box cats talk about Nietzsche.

The humorist Roy Blount is right. Cats never got over being an object of worship in ancient Egypt. They still think wistfully of Bast, the cat goddess; body of a woman, head of a cat.

Ancient Egypt, by the way, was the last place I am aware cats were known to fetch. Hunters used boomerangs to stalk game birds for food and leashed cats were released to retrieve the fallen prey.

The only game cats ever offer humans today is an occasional mouse head, a few bird feet.

I don't even think cats live up to their reputation as hunters. Several days ago, I was seated at the dining room table when I noticed a single gossamer thread descending from the ceiling. At the end with its legs splayed, hung a spider. By and by, the insect lowered itself to within a foot of the carpet and even closer to the cat resting on it.

The cat reared up, poised to pounce and took a deep breath that sucked the hapless spider into its nostril. After some snuffling and pawing, the spider was dislodged and the cat gazed about triumphantly as though it had actually planned to snare its prey by such an unconventional tactic.

Cats are supposed to be able to "mouse." It is instinctive, I am told. I gave my trio of felines a week to ferret out a field mouse hiding in the cabinet space beneath and adjoining my kitchen sink. Not only did they fail to catch the mouse, but when I finally resorted to a trap, it was all I could do to keep them from getting at the bait.

No cat bashing. Just the facts.

I'll keep my dog. During the recent cold snap I climbed under the covers and nuzzled a pair of frozen feet against the warm, furry hummock at the foot of the bed. It wasn't a cat. A few days later, when I accidentally let my hand drift over to a spot on the bedspread where one of the cats was sleeping, he (who I have dutifully fed morning and night for three years) bit me on the thumb.

You be the judge.

But Is It "Viable?"

October 3, 1993

I was on my way to lunch last week, walking two steps behind a pair of middle-aged businessmen lost in animated conversation, when the three of us happened upon an escalator under repair.

The older of the two – displaying an amazing grasp of the obvious – observed: "This escalator is not viable. We'll take the elevator."

"Not viable?" I whispered, watching them step aboard an elevator that was.

I tried to imagine them not as management consultants – which I instinctively believed them to be – but as Laurel and Hardy:

"Stanley, this escalator is not viable."

A small part of me wanted to join them "at that point in time" for the "working lunch" that it seemed their "people" had jointly and "tentatively penciled in" for the date on which they encountered the "non-viable" escalator.

How, I wondered, do such men communicate while breaking bread? How do they "interface," not merely with each other but also with the restaurant's "human resources contingent"?

Suppose the server is "motivationally deficient" or, worse, "ethically disoriented"?

What sort of "disequilibrium" interrupts lunch if there is a fly in the soup? Moreover, how would our friends convey such an unfortunate occurrence to the server?

"Waiter, just as I was preparing to 'implementate' a major 'volume reduction measure' in my 'liquid comestible,' I noticed an 'entomological specimen' of the 'Musca domestica' variety."

Now that is some nonviable soup.

What would our businessmen think if, upon asking for the waiter's opinion of the special of the day, they were told that he recommended it with "guarded optimism"?

Now that is a dangerous expression.

I would be inclined to avoid a blind date recommended with "guarded optimism."

Nor would I bet on the Buckeyes if John Cooper said he viewed his prospects with "guarded optimism."

There are two kinds of people: those who use words to illuminate and enhance the world around them and those who contribute to an ever-worsening verbal smog each time they open their mouths and belch another cloud of verbal clutter.

As I write, a man in my back yard is looking for the plug on my septic tank.

He arrived several minutes ago in a large vehicle that my truck-mechanic father once affectionately called a "honey dipper."

The man may know it better as a "human waste reduction facilitator."

I had hired him to "downsize" my "sewage infrastructure."

He parked his "mobile response unit" in the driveway, and I tried to "enhance" his "accessing" of the septic tank's "clearance mechanism."

Not wanting to give him "counterfactual" information about its location, however, I didn't pretend to be "in the loop" septicwise.

My best guesses at the location proved "factually inoperative." And the long-stemmed metal probe he used was "operationally dysfunctional."

A "dicensus" of opinion emerged. He thought it might be near the pine tree; I thought it closer to the buckeye.

He eventually found the clearing mechanism and, after employing the proper "procedural safeguards," began the "functional utilization" of his honey-dipping hose, which made – as Ross Perot might indelicately put it – a big sucking sound.

When he "finalized" his work, he handed me a bill for $202, me being the "end user" (in more ways than one) of the "sewage infrastructure."

I signed and presented him with a "negotiable fiduciary instrument."

I hope he doesn't cash it until tomorrow.

It may not be viable.

Love: Just Another Allergy

July 18, 1993

If new love were a fever – which in many ways it is – a thermometer could tell us when the danger that it might prove fatal had passed.

But we still would have other ways of knowing that the wonderful and clinically observable symptoms probably would not return: The vacuum cleaner would make annoying little clattering noises as it sucked up not rose petals strewn about the bedroom carpeting but toenail clippings. Candles once squandered over leisurely dinners would be prudently tucked away for power outages. Pablo Neruda's poetry would give way to Jay Leno's monologue.

A recent book exploring the subject, Helen Fisher's *Anatomy of Love*, suggests that over time (usually 18 months to three years) we undergo a physiological blunting of sensitivity – actual systemic changes that keep us from staying wild-crazy in love for longer than is good for us.

Fisher's suggestion somewhat reinforces the medical premise I think is at the heart of male-female relationships: We are allergic to each other – men to women, women to men.

I believe it.

If I went to an allergist and let him play pincushion with my back, subjecting me to samplings of everything from household dust to horsehair and common mold, the large welt the size of a pie plate would represent women.

There is nothing sexist about my premise. Women would react the same.

So, given the likelihood that all indications point to an allergy, we might naturally try to minimize contact with the offending agent.

After all, when we spy a poison-ivy plant, our first instincts are not to roll in it, eat it, stuff it into our gym shorts and go play handball.

Yet that is what we do with love. We feel a little dizziness, mild palpitations, insomnia and confusion (if love were a drug, the Food and Drug

Administration would confiscate and destroy it) – and what do we do?

We're like certain dogs when they find a sun-ripened road kill – we just have to roll in it.

We're snake-bit, so to speak.

If we were really bitten, we would need a lifesaving dose of serum cultivated by giving a horse almost enough snake venom to kill it.

Instead, our body, unaided, begins to build an immunity to our allergy: We stop blushing and drooling on our shoe tops. Our heart rate returns to normal. The dizziness ceases.

Having developed the immunity, we may decide to legally formalize our relationship with the snake – make it permanent.

This is a mistake. As often as not, we do not reach this decision because of the promise of a lasting, nonfatal coexistence but because of the confusion, dizziness and palpitations that were present when fangs first hit flesh.

We ought to be able to live out our lives in quiet contentment without a routine jolt from all those old symptoms. We, after all, survived the snakebite; we kissed the air bag and lived. Chastened and grateful, we might even sense that God wanted us to live (if perhaps a bit less clamorously than we had been living).

But, no, we have to go back to the woodpile where we had first disturbed a sleeping copperhead and see whether we can find – who knows? – perhaps a timber rattler.

It starts all over again: Our stomach churns. Our palms feel clammy. We can't catch our breath. And, instead of finding a shady spot to rest quietly until help arrives, we insist on running around like idiots, telling our friends how awful it feels to be freshly bitten. We might even hold the snake by the tail so they can get a good look at it.

Things quiet down after a while, and we listen a little when everyone tells us that our heart probably couldn't stand another jolt like that.

Soon enough, though, we start rubbing the scar, begin thinking about how, when the sunlight hit that coiled serpent in a certain way, it looked, well, almost...

The woodpile starts to seem inviting all over again.

The Worrier

July 8, 1992

She has furrowed the brows of the cardiologist, internist and respiratory specialist. They fret over the clot that caused the stroke, the bewilderingly stubborn lungs, the heart that stopped beating two weeks ago. She, on the other hand, is worried about the geraniums and birds.

We were 600 miles away, vacationing on the North Carolina Outer Banks, when the call came. A telephone that rings before sunrise rarely carries glad tidings.

In a mental fog, I threw off the covers and tried to recall the location of the telephone. When you rent from strangers, you are a hostage to their notions of convenience.

Debra beat me to the receiver. Her disbelieving gasp conveyed the message. Her mother, Mary, had been rushed to the hospital. Emergency-room doctors had immediately placed her on a respirator. Details were sketchy.

By the time we made it back to Columbus, a clearer picture had emerged of the problems and the tribute they had exacted.

The paramedics who went to her aid at 4 a.m. knew immediately that she was suffering a heart attack.

"What do you remember about it?" I asked her a few days ago.

She recalled disarming the security system and opening the front door so the squad attendants could get in to help her. As they began to work, one of the paramedics asked why she had waited so long to summon help. Before she lost consciousness, she heard the command "Breathe! Breathe!" then "We're losing her!"

The family assembled in the waiting room of the coronary-care unit at Mount Carmel East Hospital for the vigil.

Her relatives wanted to know how serious the heart attack had been.

Mary wanted to know whether her granddaughter had finally made up her mind about a new bathing suit.

They wanted to know the long-term prognosis.

Mary wanted to apologize for ending up in the hospital while her daughter was on vacation.

They wanted to know what rehabilitation would be needed to return strength and mobility to her left side.

Mary wanted to know whether anyone had watered her geraniums and filled the bird feeder.

Mary had the good fortune to be born amid a group of eight loving and attentive siblings. Their diligent concern takes them daily to the hospital. Their strength in numbers has been such that the only thing lacking for a family reunion at Mount Carmel is covered dishes.

Armed with Mary's home security code, I trekked over to her condo from the hospital room while she and her daughter visited. Not long before we had arrived, chest pains had sent nurses scurrying for the nitroglycerin.

The geraniums seemed healthy enough, but I filled a pitcher anyway and gave them a drink. The bird feeder was empty.

I think Mary knows perfectly well what she is doing. We go to her hospital room wringing our hands, fretting at the monitors that measure her heartbeat. She, reading our concern, gives us something to think about other than her. She tells us she is worried about not being able to show up for all of the volunteer work she routinely does.We tell her that someone will pinch-hit for her.

On a day when her pulse rate climbed alarmingly to the 160-170 range, she was asking after the welfare of the dog. She knows that our mutt, Maxie, is epileptic, and she had wanted to look after her while we were on vacation. Mary's doctor wisely counseled against it.

"She worries about everyone but herself," her sister whispered to me as we left the hospital room a few days ago.

Mary knows the gravity of her condition and the risks that the future holds before she is out of the woods. She loves us, but we are a bit like the awkward pioneer husband in the old westerns at the moment when labor pains begin. What was the midwife's command? "Lucas, you get out of here now. Go boil some water."

Go water the geraniums.

Banjo Man

April 26, 1992

I hauled my father's four-string banjo down from the shelf the other night. It was piled huggermugger in the closet with an ancient zither, a warped autoharp, a fiddle and 27 rolls of holiday wrapping paper.

It is a peculiar little instrument, his banjo. It has a short, skinny neck and an oversized head. Time has tarnished the brackets and loosened the tuning pegs. The strings are so old, they carry almost no tonal coloration.

My father played that banjo on the Grand Ole Opry. It brought down the house – two standing ovations. He probably would have played all night if Ernest Tubb hadn't been standing in the wings frowning at his wristwatch.

Of course, my father played the Opry only in his sleep.

"He used to have dreams that he could play the hell out of that thing," my mother, laughing, confided a few days ago. "He never did."

But between snores he took bows at Ryman Auditorium, showing Earl Scruggs how to master a particularly difficult run, signing autographs.

Fact is, everything my father played on the banjo sounded more or less like *Old MacDonald Had a Farm*. That tune and *Little Brown Jug* were the extent of his repertoire.

"Mary Lou," he would call to my mother, "get my banjo. I want to play something for Mike. What do you want to hear?"

"How about a little bit of *Old MacDonald*?" I would oblige.

"Yeah, that's a good old number," he would say admiringly of my choice. "Then maybe after that I'll do, oh, say, *Little Brown Jug*."

My mother liked to tease him after he bought the banjo and began practicing the only two songs he ever learned.

"Listen, and tell me what this is," he would call to her, ripping into *Old MacDonald*.

"*Little Brown Jug?*" she would venture when he finished.

My father was versatile. He could play *Little Brown Jug* and *Old MacDonald* on tenor guitar as well as tenor banjo.

Unfortunately, he stored the guitar on a shelf in the laundry room, and one day the heat and moisture got the best of it. The top peeled away like the sole on a hobo's shoe, and for two or three days my father walked around the house looking as if the dog had died.

It was not too long after that he decided to try his hand, or mouth as it were, at harmonica. When I was a tyke, he showed me how to make a poor man's kazoo using waxed paper and a pocket comb. He came to regret it, I think, after listening to me blow saliva and dandruff through *Jesus Loves Me* for the 237th time.

He bought the harmonica because my uncle Jim had purchased one and quickly learned to play *Can I sleep in Your Barn Tonight, Mister?*

He attacked the harmonica with a vengeance. It won. No matter what he played, it sounded like a cat being spayed without benefit of anesthesia. He gave up on harmonica after a mysterious saboteur blew about 4 ounces of half-chewed Lance peanut-butter crackers into it and fouled the reeds. Wasn't I.

Curious thing about my father: He had a marvelous singing voice. He could sing barbershop beautifully. His imitations of the big-band crooners were flawless. Thus, I never understood why he couldn't leave well enough and banjos alone.

When he died in 1978, my mother asked me whether I wanted the banjo.

There are several memories of my father that give me pain. The Gypsies are fond of saying, "You have to dig real deep to bury your daddy." By now I should have struck oil, water or China.

But the banjo invited neither remorse nor regret. I cannot look at it without smiling. I cannot look at it without seeing my father in his dreams, up on the stage of the Grand Ole Opry. He is nattily attired in a turquoise western suit embroidered with wild stallions. He tips his hat to the crowd. Men cheer. Women cry. He steps to the microphone and speaks:

"Bet y'all would like to hear a little *Old MacDonald* now, wouldn't you?"

The house goes wild.

Sports Trivia Madness

July 24, 1989

Dante blew a great opportunity when he failed to make a sports call-in show part of the fifth circle of hell. I have been trapped for hours out on the road when the only clear channel I can get features a never-ending procession of mushwits pondering the nuances of the slam-dunk. It is perhaps the only staple of radio programming that makes CB chatter literate by comparison.

Caller No. 1: Honey, how 'bout getting me another brewski and, uh...What? I'm on the air. Sorry, Stump. I was just havin' my main squeeze get me a beer. Hey, listen, man, how you doin'?

Stump: Fine.

Caller No. 1: That's great, dude. I love your show. You're the best. I got a baseball question for you.

Stump: Shoot.

Caller No. 1: A batter has two strikes on him. Pitcher throws a third strike. Batter swings, misses, but here's the thing. The ball gets stuck in the catcher's mask. Since the catcher didn't really catch it, can the batter run to first? And if he does, since the ball is stuck, is he out if the catcher runs him down with his face?

Stump: American League or National?

Caller No. 1: Gee. I never thought about that.

Stump: Makes all the difference in the world. Next call. You're on Sports Chatter With Stump.

Caller No. 2: Stumper, buddy. This is Bruno. Got a boxing question. Muhammad Ali used to do a thing called the rope-a-dope. Has anyone else ever used it successfully against a heavyweight fighter?

Stump: Robin Givens. Next caller.

Caller No. 3: Stump, what do you think it's going to take before synchronized swimming gets the public attention it truly deserves?

Stump: Full frontal nudity. Sharks, maybe. Next caller.

Caller No. 4: Is this Stump?

Stump: There's only one.

Caller No. 4: Naw, c'mon. I never get through on your show. This really *you*?

Stump: For this I left Boise?

Caller No. 4: OK, man. Hey, listen. I'm calling from a bar. This guy and me want you to settle a sports question. He says Kevin Mitchell is going to be the greatest home-run hitter of all time. I say the Babe was the best, even if Maris broke his record. My question is this: If the Babe was playing today, would he be leading Kevin Mitchell in home runs?

Stump: Probably not. Your bat speed starts to slow down a lot after you turn 85.

Caller No. 4: Yeah, I guess so.

Stump: Next call.

Caller No. 5: Stump, my man. Got a question. What do they call that sport down in Acapulco where those guys jump off those cliffs into a little pool of water?

Stump: Stupid seems to cover it pretty well. Next caller.

Caller No. 6: Stump. Baseball trivia, pal. If a game goes into extra innings and it is still being played at 2 a.m. when we switch to Daylight Savings Time, does that extra hour go into the official record book?

Stump: American League or National?

Caller No. 6: I don't know about that. Let me get back to you.

Stump: Next call.

Caller No. 7: How 'bout them Buckeyes!

Stump: How 'bout 'em. Next call.

Caller No. 8: Stump. What do you think is Michael Jordan's greatest asset?

Stump: His pituitary gland.

Caller No. 9: Baseball question. Batter's at the plate. Runner on first. The manager signals to the catcher for a pick-off. But the first baseman misses the signal, so when the pitcher wheels and throws the ball hits the first baseman right on the bean. He falls on the ball unconscious. How far is the runner allowed to advance?

Stump: Day game or night?

Caller No. 9: I don't know.

Stump: Next caller.

Caller No. 10: Stump. My boyfriend plays softball four nights a week. Now, I like the game, but *four* nights a week. I don't want to seem like a spoilsport, but I'm just wondering how I could get more out of Tuesday, Wednesday, Thursday and Saturday nights?

Stump: What's your home phone number?

Seventy Million Burgers

September 20, 1990

For the past several days I have been attempting to sleuth out the answer to a question that has been driving me nuts for years: Just who is it, at the international headquarters of McDonald's, who counts the burgers sold?

I tried to find out several months ago and was ping-ponged around the Oak Brook, Ill., home office until tersely informed that such information was "proprietary." Again, last week, I began my search anew. I got as close as leaving a voice message with the computer guru in the marketing department before being shuffled back down to customer relations. I am still waiting for them to tell me, once again, that the information is "proprietary." But this time, while waiting, I have been thinking.

His name is Horton Quimby or Quimby Horton, something that causes confusion in the boardroom and amusement in the mail room. He prefers bow ties, his favorite being the red one with the tiny golden arches, for he is, if nothing else, a company man. He wears a green eyeshade. A No. 2 pencil rides next to an ear that has sprouted what appears to be a small tuft of steel wool. The only palpable evidence of the stress of his job is the flecks of dried Maalox at the corners of a mouth set in perpetual scorn.

He is the sort of man who knows he owns exactly 73 pairs of socks, having disposed of the stray green argyle after puzzlement over its lost mate's fate began keeping him awake nights.

When his superiors are stumped trying to recall his name, they simply bark into the intercom, "Get me The Counter."

Twelve gray telephones are lined like plebes at inspection across the top of a desk that holds nothing else save a fat hard-bound ledger that weighs nine pounds more than his dog, Cyril.

They ring continually. He long ago learned the trick of answering two at once, scrunching his neck to hold both receivers against his shoulders in a way that makes him resemble a small vulture being treated for whiplash.

"Pascagoula?" he confirms. "Hold a moment until I get Tarzana."

There are hundreds of men and women in the employ of his company who make more money and wield far more power than he. But Quimby Pangbourn Horton is the only man alive who, at any given moment, can recite the exact number of McDonald's hamburgers that have been sold the world over.

"Seventy-one billion, six hundred forty-one million, eight hundred fifty-six thousand, nine hundred and three," he once sputtered to a baffled manager of a west Chicago McDonald's who had neglected to update a sign deficiently proclaiming "over 60 billion sold" on the day Quimby dropped in for a Big Mac.

"You are supposed to change the sign with the achievement of each new 10-billion hamburger increment," he tersely informed the startled fellow. "We have sold more than 70 billion."

On the Sunday after McDonald's topped 70 billion, Quimby took his dog, Cyril, for a ride in the country. When they reached a pasture where a small herd of feeder cattle stood huddled under a tree, Quimby stopped the car and asked his uncomprehending companion, "Cyril, do you know how many head of beef cattle have given their all for McDonald's? Fourteen million. Think of that. Imagine New York City populated by nothing but steers."

Only twice in all his years with McDonald's has Quimby Horton ever panicked on the job. Once, when he found himself trapped on a corporate elevator with 11 Ronald McDonald trainees, he hyperventilated. He has no patience for the clowns and anthropomorphic cheeseburgers who make up his company's mascots.

His second panic attack came in 1981, when the Breezewood, Pa., McDonald's gave him a half-number in their daily count.

"You can't have a half-number," he screamed into the receiver. reaching for his Maalox.

"We had a half-burger left on the grill at the end of the day," he was told.

In great agitation, Quimby fled his office, drove to the nearest McDonald's and commanded, "I want half of a cheeseburger, and I want you to destroy the rest." When the dawdling clerk asked obligatorily, "Would you like some fries with that?" Quimby had to be restrained from strangling him.

"Seventy billion," he whistled one recent night as he pulled the covers up to his chin. "Cyril, that is 13 burgers for every man, woman and child on the face of this earth."

Then he paused to release a small belch of contentment tasting of two all-beef patties, special sauce, lettuce, cheese, pickles, onions on a sesame seed bun – and Maalox – before smugly whispering, "And I counted all of them."

My Religion, My Business

December 1, 1989

In the morning mail, not many days ago, I received a letter from an acquaintance of my youth telling me to "get right with God." It was but one of three recent missives nudging me toward the altar, each more unsettling than its predecessor if only because, collectively, they suggested some ominous public knowledge concerning my cholesterol level or brake linings about which I remain blissfully ignorant.

One's religion, like one's underwear, seem to me a personal matter, and I resent, in the case of either the former or the latter, the urgings of folks to try theirs on for size.

I do not attend the church of my choice, mostly because I have no choice. I scribble "none" on forms that inquire about my religious preference. If, in some eyes, that brands me a heathen, I will live with that scourge rather than the yoke of a denomination that smugly believes itself the one true church.

When I am invited to join this congregation or that, I usually paraphrase the late Groucho Marx, protesting that I would not want to belong to a church that would have me as a member.

When I was 5, my mother sent me to a vacation Bible school operated by the Friends Church. I recall little of it, save a fellow who demonstrated to his callow charges how whiskey could be used to fry an egg.

I did not stay long with the Friends Church, in large measure because of my grandmother's belief that the stairway to heaven began at the steps of the Pentecostal church. She had no use for lukewarm religions.

Catholicism was a dark mystery full of ritual and candles. From my classmates in Sunday school I learned that all nuns were bald, and many of them kidnapped children to be shipped off to a life of bondage in Vatican City dungeons.

It stuns me now to think of the brutal religious prejudices and stereotyping that colored my childhood. I was a teen-ager before I knew that "Jew" could be used as something other than a verb.

When I was old enough to "just say no" to fundamentalism, I did.

In the service, my dog tags were stamped "other" in the space reserved for religion. I went unbaptized until a chaplain convinced me that there are no atheists in foxholes and, not far from my own, sprinkled me with water.

I would later be baptized Catholic, but not before taking catechism from a priest fresh from a stint of several years as chaplain at the Ohio Penitentiary. I liked him if only because I imagined he had a more enlightened view of what constituted actual sin than most of his brothers in the faith.

As the years passed, I found myself questioning the policies and doctrines of the church. My views were not much different from those of a young priest whose unhappy fate it was to be assigned to my church as assistant to a pastor who loathed religious liberalism and scorned its proponents as "a la carte Catholics." When a schism developed between warring factions in the parish, I leaped into it.

For a while I was referred to as a "lapsed Catholic," a semantic brickbat combining failure and grace in much the same manner of "idiot savant." Truth be known, I don't know what I am. Former fundamentalist. Ex-Episcopalian. Lapsed Catholic.

I firmly believe that there is a greater force than humankind somewhere out there. I think that deep in their bones most people do. Not many folks brace themselves for major surgery by phoning up Madalyn Murray O'Hair.

I suppose I should think about that force, whatever it is, at times other than when the car skids on the ice, the fever thermometer climbs, or the house timbers begin to shudder during a tornado warning.

On the other hand, if I insist that its grace is inextricably entwined with an earthly interpretation – with annual dues and middlemen (middle-women are denied access to the pulpit in some faiths) and bumper stickers – then I have committed the ultimate sin by making it mortal.

A "Hotbed of Synchronized Swimming"

August 23, 1993

St. Peter hauled Woody Hayes and Bear Bryant before God's Tribunal of Angels last week for fighting; and, from the size of the crowd on hand to witness the affair, one would have thought it was the Sugar Bowl.

Both sides of the heavenly chamber of justice were lined with cheering, jeering, hoo-hawing fans of Alabama and Ohio State who waved placards that proclaimed "Roll Tide" and "Go Bucks."

A hush fell over those assembled when St. Peter cried, "All rise. The First Council of the Devout and All-Righteous Tribunal of Angels is now in session. Bow now before the immaculate countenance of the king of kings."

At this, the supreme judge entered, with King Solomon close at his heels and holding the flowing train of the deity's long robe.

"If it please the Holy Ghost," St. Peter read from a bill of particulars as God took his seat, "the tribunal would like to call before the altar of justice Wayne Woodrow 'Woody' Hayes and Paul 'Bear' Bryant."

"Bring them forth," God said without looking up from the docket list before him.

Hayes' left eye was puffy and discolored, and, when he smiled toward the assembled throng in scarlet sweaters, he revealed a gap where an incisor once had been.

Part of Bryant's upper lip was swollen to the size of a frankfurter, and his forehead was scratched where it had not quite dodged a knuckle adorned with a Rose Bowl ring.

"It has come to my attention," the Lord said, sighing in exasperation, "that you two have been fighting again."

Hayes and Bryant fidgeted nervously, hands clasped before them, and pretended to be engrossed in something on their shoe tops.

"You want to go first, Woody?" God invited.

"Doggone it, Lord," Woody began, "he insulted the good name of the finest football school in the whole world. Couldn't let that happen – no, sir – without giving him a licking. Come up on him like Grant took Richmond. You remember that, God – don't you? – when Grant..."

"Enough," God interjected. "Mr. Bryant, I presume you have a version of this."

"Aw, Lord," Bryant responded, "weren't nothing to speak of. I just told him how proud he ought to be that some sports commentator at the U.S. Olympic Festival had finally accorded Ohio State the position of athletic excellence it deserves by describing it – and I'm quoting now, Lord – as 'a hotbed of synchronized swimming.'"

A hiss issued from the Buckeye gallery, a few guffaws from the Alabama side.

"Well," the Lord said, turning to Woody, "is it true what the commentator said?"

"Oh, yeah, Your Reverence," Bryant interrupted, giggling. "They do some real smashmouth dog paddlin' up there in Buckeye country. Look like the June Taylor dancers in nose clips."

"I'm gonna bust him, Lord," Woody said, fuming.

Solomon gaveled the pair to silence.

The Lord then turned to Woody, asking, "Because you obviously think that the commentator's remark was made at the expense of OSU's football program, perhaps you would care to tell us when the football team last enjoyed the position of national esteem now held by OSU synchronized swimming?"

"Doggone it, Lord," Woody protested.

"Or basketball?" the Lord continued.

"Men's or women's?" Woody asked.

"Make any difference?" the Lord said.

"Could be either. Why, the philosophy department's teaching assistants' team even looks pretty good when compared."

"That's pretty mean, Lord," Woody responded.

"I could have gone on to fencing, field hockey or the ag department's milking team.

"Tell you what: I'm suspending both of your TV viewing rights through September. And, Woody, you might learn something about taking your lumps gracefully by studying Earle Bruce. He has found his niche and is returning to Ohio State as a commentator and analyst for the school's most revered sport."

"You don't say," Woody mused.

Bryant smiled broadly: "I didn't know Earle Bruce knew that much about synchronized swimming."

"The Attack of the Morning People"

October 1, 1989

I keep waiting to hear a TV promotion that goes something like this:

"They were cheerful, relentlessly cheerful. Tonight, the world premiere of the NBC-TV movie *Attack of the Morning People*, starring Sandy Duncan, Mary Tyler Moore and – in his dramatic debut – Willard Scott.

Here is Willard Scott, up before the sun, broadcasting on location in Charleston, S.C., amid the devastation wreaked by the killer hurricane Hugo:

"Hey, we're having a great time here in Charleston."

Willard is holding a baby squirrel NBC rescued from the storm. He says it is doing well. The squirrel appears on the verge of expiring from terminal optimism. But:

"Hey, we're having a great time here. Your house blew away? No insurance? Hey. Rub ol' Willard's head for luck."

He didn't actually utter the latter quote. But he thought about it.

Morning people are proud of their label. They call themselves "morning people."

"Isn't it great to be alive," they will tell you at 6:45 a.m. as they tape *Family Circus* to their refrigerators (having already taped *Ziggy* to their foreheads).

It is not *great* to be alive at 6:45 a.m. At 6:45 a.m. I am still thinking about throwing myself off the Broad Street bridge, stopped only by the certain knowledge that I would be thwarted by some morning person playing Henry Travers to Jimmy Stewart a la *It's a Wonderful Life*.

"You see. Mike, you've really had a wonderful life. Don't you see what a mistake it would be to throw it away?"

"Outta my way, Clarence."

Splash! Fade to black. Roll credits.

Morning people cannot help themselves. It is a disease. But with early detection and treatment, they can be cured. If you are worried that you or someone you love is becoming a morning person, consider these seven early warning signs:

1. Smiles before noon and often when alone.

2. Whistles or hums along with Muzak while riding elevator up to office.

3. Thinks the glass is half full.

4. Actually believes it *will* clear up before noon.

5. Likes to say, "Ooooo. Did we get up on the wrong side of the bed this morning?" (At 6:45 a.m. there is no right side).

6. Dots the letter "i" with smile face or heart.

7. Wonders why *The Dispatch* never picked up the comic strip *Love Is*.

Choose for yourself. Which group do you want to be a part of?

Famous Morning People: Sandy Duncan, Mary Tyler Moore, Willard Scott, Howdy Doody, David Hartman, Leo Buscalgia, Mary Lou Retton, Dr. Robert Schuller, Dr. Norman Vincent Peale. Fred Rogers.

Famous Night People: Henry VIII, Mark Twain, W.C. Fields, H.L. Mencken, Edwin R. Newman, Fran Lebowitz, C. Everett Koop, Sean Penn, Don Rickles.

OK, OK. So I forgot Manson. Picky, picky, picky.

Often, morning people can be identified simply by the career choices they make. Consider:

Morning People Occupations: Kindergarten Teacher, TV meteorologist, funeral director, welcome wagon hostess, Ronald McDonald, airline steward(ess), Miss America contestant, company spokesman. (The guy who let the *Exxon Valdez* run aground was, regrettably, a night person. The guy explaining what a wonderful job Exxon is doing with the cleanup is a morning person).

Night People Occupations: Hit man, relief pitcher, bookie, taxi drier, city editor, linebacker, country music singer.

Morning people thank the time-and-temperature recording, wonder what ever happened to the polka and already have finished this year's Christmas shopping.

Morning people are always optimists. Put a road apple in their Christmas stocking, and they start looking around for a pony. Night people tend toward pessimism.

To paraphrase famous night person J. Robert Oppenheimer, a morning person *thinks* this is the best of all possible worlds; the night person *knows* it.

One Wife Too Many

September 20, 1993

My wife and my ex-wife are each other's best friend. How they have bonded so intensely is beyond me, but it is as though they were strangers who, by chance meeting on an ocean cruise, discovered they suffered from the same rare and intractable fungus, a scourge with symptoms so morbidly unpleasant that they can be truly appreciated only by another similarly afflicted soul.

It is a bond that has strengthened so significantly over the past two or three years that I occasionally feel like something of an interloper when they become lost in animated conversation.

Last week, when my ex-wife required foot surgery and was advised to stay off of the fresh cast for several days, my wife not only decided that someone should cook for her, but also that I should be that person.

The arrangement between wives current and ex seems surprising to some, amusing to a few.

"This is Mike Harden's first wife," as a mutual friend loves to introduce them at a restaurant we frequent, "and this is Mike Harden's second wife."

Not long ago in that restaurant, the three of us ran into a couple none of us had seen since my ex and I were divorced. The explanation of the reconfigured relationships left them nodding in somewhat baffled acknowledgement and momentarily silent.

You figure it out.

At the marrow of their firm friendship is the bond that they share a common enemy: me.

Together, they have an abiding interest in the children they consider their own either by blood or marriage. And it is naturally advantageous to the children that they do not have to feel caught up in any of the wars for allegiance sometimes waged between biological and step-parents.

It has gotten to the point that rather than have the children spend half the holidays driving back and forth between homes to ensure that no feelings are bruised, my ex- and current wives simply plan one big celebration.

Funny thing. Four or five years ago, my current wife would silently indulge my occasional carping about my ex. I refrain from such petty sniping now because my wife has taken all the fun out of it. If I harp about some real or imagined past offense, the new wife leaps in – sword drawn – not merely to defend her predecessor, but to praise her better nature in a way that sounds for all the world as though she is recommending a prospective blind date.

This baffles me, for I have been in situations where circumstance has forced another's ex-spouse and current mate to occupy the same room for a limited time. It is a little like being on an elevator whose only other occupants are a mongoose and a cobra.

They trade venomous glances and hiss unprintable things into the ears of anyone who listens.

But all is sweetness and light between the former and current Mrs. Hardens. It has reached the point that when one or the other is trying to convince me of something, the other routinely chimes in, "You listen to her, now. What she is saying is right, and you know it." To sit between the two when this is going on is akin to watching a Wimbledon match – and sometimes like being the ball.

The danger to my humble defenses is that, thanks to their unshakable alliance and the resultant sharing of notes, knowledge and strategies, they collectively possess 22 years of experience at outsmarting me.

It makes it impossible to recycle some old marital sleight of hand because of the inevitable conferencing that will unmask it as something I had tried 20 years ago.

What bothers me most is that jealousy is the furthest thing from their minds. It is as though they sat down and earnestly discussed the subject of their joint consternation and determined that there simply isn't enough of substance to quibble over.

Order Form

Simply fill out the coupon below and mail to:

Mike Harden
P.O. Box 1235
Dublin, OHio 43017

Enclosed is my check or money order for $11.95 plus $1 for postage and handling for each copy of Among Friends. Please send _____ copy(ies).
Ohio residents please add 5.75 percent state sales tax.

Mail to:

NAME _____
STREET ADDRESS _____
CITY _____STATE _____ZIP_____